THE BUDDHA *said* WHAT?!

HANDLING FRUSTRATION LIKE A BUDDHIST

ANONGPA PAYANAN

Notes

For more information, email mybuddhistway@gmail.com.

ISBN: 979-8-89109-259-4 - paperback
ISBN: 979-8-89109-262-4 - ebook

DEDICATION

I would like to dedicate this book to the following people:

My parents

To my beloved parents, even though you now reside in heaven, your eternal love, unwavering support, and the freedom you bestowed upon me continue to shape my life. I am forever grateful for the good life you provided and the values you instilled in me. Though you may be physically absent, I believe you watch over me from above, guiding and protecting me. This dedication is a tribute to your enduring presence in my heart and the immeasurable impact you have had on my life.

My son

To my cherished son, you have consistently shown unwavering goodness and have been an exemplary child in every way. Your kindness, compassion, and unwavering positivity have brought immeasurable joy and pride into my life. You have always been a source of inspiration, reminding me of the beauty and innocence that reside within us all. This dedication is a testament to your remarkable character and serves as a heartfelt tribute to the extraordinary person you have become.

TABLE OF CONTENTS

INTRODUCTION

Dear All,

I decided to write this book after observing the significant challenges and struggles endured by many people around me. From job losses and the loss of loved ones to divorce, separations from family, and health issues, these hardships have deeply impacted their well-being. Inspired by their struggles, I offer insights and guidance rooted in Buddhism to help navigate life's obstacles and find inner peace.

Having been born and raised in Thailand, a country where Buddhism plays a significant role in the culture, traditions, and daily lives of its people, I have been practicing meditation since a young age. Despite studying Buddhism in school, it was only through dedicated meditation practice that I truly began to grasp the fundamental roots of its teachings.

Just like everyone else, my life has been graced with imperfections and challenges. Yet I've come to embrace them as essential elements that make the human experience truly remarkable. They grant me a clearer view of life's reality and inspire me to support others in overcoming obstacles and finding happiness. My ultimate goal is to empower individuals from all walks of life to adapt well to challenges and cultivate inner peace.

This book intricately connects Buddhist wisdom with contemporary life. It presents valuable insights from Buddhist teachings that can benefit anyone seeking solutions in life. Whether you're Buddhist or from another faith, facing challenges or aiding others, these teachings cultivate profound life wisdom and peace, enabling resilient navigation of obstacles.

I warmly invite you to embark on this journey with an open heart and mind, ready to explore Buddhist thoughts and practical applications. I hope that this book serves as a guiding light, providing solace, inspiration, and practical strategies to help you find meaning, healing, and inner peace in your personal journey.

With gratitude and warm wishes,
Anongpa Payanan

CHAPTER 1

THE CYCLE OF REBIRTH

H AVE YOU ever wondered what life after death might look like? Do you believe in the separation of the body and soul? Could it be possible that after death, the physical body ceases to exist while the soul continues its journey in a new body?

Lastly, do you accept the concept of rebirth?

What's Rebirth?

Rebirth is a core belief in Buddhism, and while it shares similarities with reincarnation, there are distinct differences between the two concepts. Reincarnation generally refers to the belief that the same soul or spirit is reborn into a new body after death. In contrast, rebirth refers to the idea that consciousness continues after death and is reborn into a new body based on the karmic actions of the previous life. While the concept of rebirth is primarily a matter of faith and belief rather than something that can be empirically proven by scientific evidence, there have been several scientific studies conducted in Asia related to the concept of reincarnation and rebirth. These have been particularly popular in countries like India, Sri Lanka, and Thailand, where Buddhism, a philosophy that believes in rebirth, is prevalent. While these studies do not definitively prove the existence of reincarnation or rebirth, they do provide intriguing evidence that the soul, or consciousness, may continue after death and travel from one body to another. Here are some examples of such studies:

The Work of Dr. Ian Stevenson: Dr. Ian Stevenson was a Canadian-born American psychiatrist who spent over forty years researching cases of children who claimed to remember their past lives. Dr. Stevenson traveled extensively to Asia and other parts of the world to interview children and their families who claimed to have past-life memories. Then, he verified the details of those memories by conducting investigations at the locations they claimed to have lived in their past lives. He also examined birthmarks and birth defects that were said to be related to the past lives of the children. Although Stevenson's work has been criticized by some scientists for its lack of empirical evidence and methodological flaws, he is still considered by many to be a pioneer in the field of reincarnation research. His work is highly respected in the scientific community and has been published in numerous academic journals.

The Study by Professor Erlendur Haraldsson: Professor Erlendur Haraldsson, a well-known psychologist from Iceland, carried out extensive research on reincarnation and rebirth across various countries. One of his studies on reincarnation was conducted in Sri Lanka in the 1980s, where he interviewed twenty-five children who claimed to remember their past lives. He conducted detailed interviews with the children, their families, and the individuals who they claimed to have been their previous selves. He also compared the information provided by the children with the actual biographical data of their claimed previous selves. He found that the children's memories of their past lives were often accurate and included specific details about their previous lives that could not have been known by anyone in their current lives. Some skeptics argued that the information about these past lives could have been obtained through normal means, such as through the media or overhearing conversations. However, Professor Haraldsson found that many of the children had no access to the media and that the details they provided could not have been obtained through overheard conversations.

The Work of Dr. Jim Tucker: Dr. Jim Tucker is a child psychiatrist and researcher who has conducted several studies on the subject of reincarnation. Building upon the groundbreaking work of Dr. Ian Stevenson, Dr. Tucker has dedicated himself to furthering research on children who possess vivid memories of their past lives. He has documented cases of children in India who claim to remember their past lives and have been able to provide specific details that were later confirmed to be true. One of his best-known cases is that of a boy named Ryan, who claimed to remember his past life as a Hollywood extra. Ryan's memories were specific and detailed, and he was able to identify several individuals who had been involved in his previous life, as well as the names of the movies he had appeared in. Dr. Tucker and his team conducted extensive historical research, corroborating many of the details and leading them to the conclusion that Ryan's memories were highly likely to be authentic. Dr. Tucker has also studied cases where children recall past lives involving traumatic deaths. In some cases, some of these children have birthmarks or other physical characteristics corresponding to injuries sustained by the person they remember being in their previous life. While further research is necessary to fully understand the intricacies of reincarnation, he believes that these cases provide compelling evidence in support of the idea that consciousness can survive beyond death and be reborn into a new body.

Professor Haraldsson's, Dr. Stevenson's, and Dr. Tucker's studies are three of many examples of scientific research that has been conducted on the topic of reincarnation and rebirth. While the results of these studies are highly debated and controversial, they hold undeniable significance in the field of parapsychology as they offer insight into the possibility of the soul continuing after death and being reborn into a new body. In this chapter, my aim is to offer you profound insights into Buddhist teachings on the cycle of rebirth and the profound consequences of karma. By delving into these teachings, we can deepen our understanding of how our actions shape our destinies and how the choices we make in this life carry forward into future existences.

Buddhist Perspectives on Rebirth and Karma

In Buddhism, the body and soul are seen as distinct entities with their own unique characteristics. The body is made up of the four elements—earth, water, wind (air), and fire—and is regarded as a temporary vessel for the soul, which is seen as the true essence that gives life to the body. To enhance your understanding of our physical existence, let's delve into an explanation of the four elements within the body. The element earth symbolizes stability and solidity, representing the physical structure of our body, including bones and muscles. Water signifies fluidity and adaptability, reflecting the presence of bodily fluids like blood that flow within us. Wind, or air, embodies movement and vitality, closely linked to our breath and the dynamic energy that sustains us. Fire represents transformation and energy, encompassing the metabolic processes in our body and generating warmth. In accordance with Buddhist beliefs, before birth, individuals exist in a state of pure consciousness without any physical form. When death comes, the body and soul separate, and the soul embarks on a new journey, being born into a new body. This continuous cycle of rebirth is a fundamental principle in Buddhist philosophy. Moreover, the new life one receives is not predetermined; instead, it is influenced by the actions and intentions of their previous life. This understanding of karma shapes the course of our existence within this timeless cycle.

It's interesting to consider why some genuinely good people encounter challenges while seemingly bad individuals prosper. Could it be that the hardships faced by the virtuous are connected to their past-life karma? In a nutshell, this idea prompts us to think about how our current actions can affect what happens to us in the future. The belief in rebirth gives us a way to understand why there are differences and inequalities in society. It is frequently noticed that some people who engage in unethical conduct appear to be favored with material wealth and prosperity, while others who live virtuously may face financial struggles and hardship. These imbalances can be linked to actions taken in their previous lives, which can impact their present circumstances. Our passions and desires are the driving forces behind the cycle of rebirth. When we cling to these desires, we continue to be caught in the cycle, experiencing both pleasure and pain. To escape this cycle and find freedom from suffering, we must let go of our attachments and develop a deep understanding of reality. This understanding leads to enlightenment, which allows us to transcend the cycle of rebirth.

Endless Cycle of Samsara

According to Buddhism, all beings are believed to be part of an unending cycle called Samsara. This cycle involves the processes of birth, death, and rebirth and is influenced by karma. Essentially, our actions have a direct impact on our future lives within this continuous cycle. This cycle is perpetuated by the accumulation of karma, which arises from one's intentions, thoughts, and actions. Karma is not viewed as a system of reward or punishment but rather as a natural law that influences one's future rebirth. Every action has its own repercussions, and the nature of one's karmic outcomes is determined by the quality of one's intentions. In the teachings of the Buddha, positive actions or good karma result in positive consequences, while negative actions or bad karma lead to negative consequences. This understanding of karma emphasizes personal responsibility and accountability for our actions, as well as the recognition that these actions have consequences beyond the present moment. As mentioned earlier, after death, the soul persists and enters the cycle of Samsara, which encompasses the experiences of all living beings. The cycle of Samsara is believed to be categorized into three realms of existence: the Desire Realm, the Form realm, and the Formless realm. These realms represent different levels of existence where a soul can be reborn. Gaining insight into these realms can deepen our understanding of the nature of existence and the causes of suffering. Further, contemplating our actions and their potential impact on our future rebirths can help us cultivate greater awareness and ethical behavior.

In the following section, we will delve deeper into each realm, providing detailed information about their characteristics and nature.

I. **The Desire Realm** is the lowest realm of existence in the cycle of Samsara. Beings who are born into this realm have a strong attachment to material and sensual pleasures, such as the desire for food, sex, and other physical pleasures. They are governed by their cravings and are often driven by their desires. Even though they enjoy sensory pleasures, they are bound by the law of impermanence. This means that their pleasures are temporary and ultimately unsatisfying. Despite their enjoyment, they still experience suffering, including physical pain and mental distress. The Desire Realm is divided into two main realms: the Happy Realm (Sugati) and the Unhappy Realm (Duggati). These realms are further divided into different sub-realms.

A. **The Happy Realm** is a realm characterized by its pleasant surroundings, beautiful colors, and sweet sounds. The beings born into this realm enjoy a relatively peaceful and content existence with little suffering or pain. The sub-realms within the Happy Realm include:

1. **Heavenly (Deva):** The Heavenly sub-realm is a realm characterized by extreme happiness, pleasure, and beauty. The Devas, or celestial beings, in this realm are believed to be blissful and godlike. They enjoy a luxurious and opulent existence, surrounded by beautiful gardens, palaces, and heavenly mansions. They are free from any kind of physical or emotional pain, suffering, or disease. However, the Devas are not

immune to suffering. The root cause of suffering in this realm is their attachment to their pleasant existence, which can lead to complacency and a lack of motivation to achieve spiritual progress. Devas may also experience fear of losing their celestial status and the resulting suffering that would entail. In Buddhist teachings, the Heavenly Sub-realm is considered to have a temporary and impermanent existence, and the Devas are believed to be subject to the cycle of rebirth like all other beings in Samsara.

2. **Jealous Gods (Asura):** The Jealous Gods sub-realm is a realm characterized by intense struggle and relentless competition. Beings in this realm, known as Asuras, are driven by their insatiable desires for power, wealth, and status. They possess a fierce and warlike nature, often engaging in conflicts with one another. Jealousy, aggression, and an unending thirst to surpass others define their existence. However, despite their formidable traits, Asuras remain trapped in suffering and the cycle of rebirth. Their discontent stems from the deep-rooted emotions of envy and jealousy.

3. **Human:** The Human sub-realm is the realm of mortals, where beings undergo a diverse range of experiences encompassing both joy and suffering. In this realm, beings possess the faculties of rational thinking, emotions, desires, and sensory perceptions. It is a realm that allows for self-awareness and the capacity to make choices that shape one's destiny. One of the main root causes of suffering in this

realm is ignorance, which leads to delusion and confusion about the true nature of reality. This can lead to attachment to transient pleasures and aversion to pain, which in turn perpetuates the cycle of suffering. Additionally, humans in this realm may also experience suffering as a result of aging, illness, and death. Despite the inherent challenges, this realm is seen as a valuable opportunity for spiritual development and advancement. By cultivating qualities like mindfulness, compassion, and wisdom, humans have the potential to transcend the causes of suffering and attain genuine happiness and inner peace. It is a realm where personal growth and spiritual transformation can take place.

B. **The Unhappy Realm** is a realm characterized by suffering and misery. The beings born into this realm experience various forms of pain, such as hunger, thirst, disease, and physical discomfort. The sub-realms within the Unhappy Realm include:

1. **Animal:** The Animal sub-realm is the realm of non-human animals. Beings in this realm are driven by instinct and have limited intellectual capacities. They are often subjected to violence and forced to live in harsh conditions. The root cause of suffering in this realm is ignorance and a lack of understanding of the nature of reality. According to Buddhist teachings, rebirth into the Animal Sub-realm is the result of negative karma from past lives. In order to escape this realm and achieve a higher level of existence, beings

must strive to cultivate positive karma through virtuous actions and mindfulness.

2. **Hungry Ghost (Preta):** The Pretas in this realm are hungry ghosts who suffer from intense hunger and thirst. They are depicted as having large stomachs and tiny mouths, which make it impossible for them to satisfy their cravings. Beings in this realm experience extreme hunger and thirst and are tormented by the sight and smell of food and water that they cannot consume. They are unable to satisfy their cravings and are tormented by their desires. The root cause of suffering in this realm is believed to be excessive greed and miserliness in their previous lives. They were unable to share their wealth and resources with others and often acted selfishly. As a result, they are reborn in the Hungry Ghost Sub-realm, where they are unable to satisfy their own needs for sustenance. In addition to hunger and thirst, they also suffer from intense feelings of loneliness, isolation, and despair. This realm is considered to be one of the lower realms of existence, where beings are trapped in a cycle of suffering and unable to make progress towards enlightenment. However, like all sub-realms, it is not permanent, and beings can eventually be reborn into a higher realm through their karmic actions.

3. **Hell:** The Hell sub-realm is the realm of intense suffering, where beings experience extreme physical and emotional pain. It is characterized by extreme heat, cold, and other forms of intense physical and mental suffering. Beings in this realm

are constantly tormented by their own negative actions and emotions. They have accumulated negative karma from their past lives, which has led them to be reborn in this realm. The root causes of suffering in this realm are hatred, anger, and jealousy. It is believed that beings in this realm can escape and be reborn into a better realm by doing good and practicing spirituality. However, escaping this realm can take many lifetimes due to the intense suffering experienced here. Overall, the root cause of suffering in both the Happy and Unhappy Realms is attachment and craving. Beings in the Happy Realm are attached to their pleasant surroundings and sensory pleasures, which can lead to disappointment and suffering when those pleasures are no longer available. Beings in the Unhappy Realm suffer from the consequences of their past negative actions and the ongoing effects of their negative karma. Both realms must practice Buddhism's teachings, such as the Four Noble Truths and the Noble Eightfold Path, which will be explored in later chapters, to cultivate virtues, wisdom, and compassion. By overcoming their attachment to desires and attaining higher realms of existence through Buddhist practices, one can achieve enlightenment and break the cycle of Samsara.

II. **The Form Realm** is the second realm of existence in the cycle of Samsara. Beings in the Form Realm experience a state of existence that is more refined than that in the Desire Realm, with a greater degree of mental and spiritual development. The Form Realm is further divided into four sub-realms that are inhabited by beings who have

ANONGPA PAYANAN

achieved various levels of meditative absorption. Each of
these sub-realms has its own unique characteristics and
levels of consciousness.

A. **The First Jhana:** The First Jhana sub-realm is
sometimes referred to as the realm of Delightful
Sustained Meditation. Beings in this realm experience
the first level of meditative absorption, which is
characterized by feelings of joy, happiness, and
equanimity. They possess a refined physical form
and enjoy a lifespan of thousands of years. Despite
their relative blissful state, they are still subject to
the cycle of rebirth as they have not yet achieved full
enlightenment.

B. **The Second Jhana:** The Second Jhana sub-realm
is also referred to as the realm of Inner Blissful
Attainment. Beings in this realm have achieved
the second level of meditative absorption, which is
characterized by a deep sense of peace and tranquility.
They possess even more refined physical forms and
experience heightened levels of joy and happiness
compared to those in the First Jhana Sub-realm.
However, despite their elevated state, they too remain
bound by the cycle of rebirth and are subject to the
impermanence of existence.

C. **The Third Jhana:** The Third Jhana sub-realm is
sometimes known as the realm of Equanimity and
Radiant Mindfulness. Beings in this realm have
achieved the third level of meditative absorption,
which is characterized by a profound sense of
equanimity and detachment. They possess an even
more refined physical form than those in the Second
Jhana Sub-realm and experience a state of perfect
contentment. While they are still subject to the cycle

of rebirth, they are closer to enlightenment than those in the First and Second Jhana Sub-realms.

D. **The Fourth Jhana:** The Fourth Jhana sub-realm is also referred to as the realm of Pure Equanimity and Sublime Abiding. Beings in this realm have achieved the fourth and highest level of meditative absorption, which is characterized by a complete absence of sensory experience and a deep state of tranquility. They possess the most refined physical form of all the Form Realm and experience the highest levels of joy and happiness. While they are still subject to the cycle of rebirth, they are much closer to achieving enlightenment and breaking free from the cycle of Samsara.

In the Form Realm, beings have progressed spiritually and are less attached to worldly desires compared to the Desire Realm. However, there is a risk of becoming attached to their elevated state and losing sight of enlightenment, leading to suffering. Despite their advancements, beings are not completely free from attachment and delusion. The root causes of suffering in this realm are still desire and ignorance, but in a more subtle and refined form. They desire a refined state of existence and mistakenly believe it to be permanent and ultimate. However, they still have residual karma to resolve before achieving complete liberation. Additionally, they experience impermanence and must confront the suffering of separation and the dissolution of their form. To overcome suffering, continuous spiritual practice and a deeper understanding of reality are necessary. Only by transcending desire and ignorance can true liberation be attained, breaking free from the cycle of Samsara.

III. **The Formless Realm** is the highest realm of existence in Buddhism. The Formless Realm is characterized by a lack of physical form and sensory experience, as beings in this realm exist purely in a formless state of consciousness. This realm is accessible only to beings who have attained a high level of spiritual development and have cultivated profound levels of meditative concentration. There are four sub-realms in the Formless Realm, each with their own unique characteristics and a progressively deeper level of meditative absorption. They are:

A. **The Realm of Infinite Space:** In this realm, beings experience a boundless, infinite space that is free of any form or materiality. The primary cause of suffering in this realm arises from attachment to the experience of boundlessness, which can result in a feeling of detachment and isolation from other beings.

B. **The Realm of Infinite Consciousness:** In this realm, beings experience a boundless, infinite consciousness that is not limited by any object or form. The root cause of suffering in this realm is attachment to the experience of boundless consciousness, which can lead to a sense of superiority over beings in lower realms.

C. **The Realm of Nothingness:** In this realm, beings experience a complete absence of any form or consciousness. The root cause of suffering in this realm is attachment to the experience of nothingness, which can lead to a sense of nihilism and a lack of purpose.

D. **The Realm of Neither Perception nor Non-Perception:** In this realm, beings experience a complete cessation of all perception and consciousness. The root cause of suffering in this realm is attachment

24

to the experience of cessation, which can lead to a sense of apathy and a lack of motivation.

While beings in the Formless Realm have achieved a highly refined state of consciousness, they are not completely free from the cycle of rebirth. Like beings in the Form Realm, they still have residual karma to work through before achieving complete liberation. The root cause of suffering in the Formless Realm is the same as in the Form Realm: desire and ignorance of the true nature of reality. However, the nature of desire and ignorance is even more subtle and refined in this realm. To overcome the root causes of suffering in the Formless Realm, beings must cultivate profound levels of meditative concentration and develop wisdom through deepening their understanding of the true nature of reality.

Attainment of Enlightenment

The ultimate goal for beings in the Formless Realm, as well as in other realms, is to transcend all desires and ignorance and attain the ultimate truth of enlightenment. By doing so, they can liberate themselves from the cycle of Samsara and find freedom from all forms of suffering. It is believed that the cycle of birth and death has no clear beginning or end, making it difficult to determine its exact time frame. Beings are driven to continue in this cycle by their own passions and desires. The path to breaking free from this cycle lies in the complete eradication of passions and desires, leading to the attainment of enlightenment. In Buddhism, ignorance of the Four Noble Truths is considered one of the primary causes of suffering. This ignorance can keep us trapped in the cycle of Samsara, preventing us from attaining true liberation. Understanding the Four Noble Truths is fundamental to Buddhist teachings, as they offer insights into the nature of suffering and the path to liberation. It is essential to grasp these truths in order to navigate the Buddhist path effectively. The First Noble Truth is the truth of suffering (Dukkha). It states that suffering is an inherent part of existence and that all beings, regardless of their social status, experience it. This includes physical and emotional pain, as well as the more subtle forms of dissatisfaction and unease that permeate our lives. The Second Noble Truth is the truth of the origin of suffering (Samudaya). It teaches that the root cause of suffering is craving and attachment, which arise from our ignorance of the true nature of reality. We cling to fleeting pleasures and desires, and when they inevitably fade away, we experience disappointment and suffering. The Third Noble Truth is the truth of the cessation of suffering (Nirodha). It teaches that the cessation of suffering is possible and that we can attain liberation from suffering by eradicating our attachment and craving. The Fourth Noble Truth is the truth of the path leading to the cessation of suffering (Magga). This path is known as the Eightfold Path and is a set of guidelines for ethical and mental development. The eight aspects of the path include right understanding, right intention, right speech, right action, right livelihood, right effort, right mindfulness, and right concentration. By following this path, we can cultivate wisdom and compassion, overcome our ignorance and cravings, and ultimately achieve liberation from suffering. In summary, the Four Noble Truths diagnose the problem of suffering, identify its root cause, present a vision of liberation from suffering, and offer a practical path to achieve that liberation. These teachings remain a source of inspiration and guidance for millions of Buddhists around the world. In Chapter 4, we will explore the Fourth Noble Truth, a vital aspect of Buddhist teachings that focuses on ending suffering and achieving liberation. By studying this chapter, you will gain a thorough understanding of the practices and principles related to the cessation of suffering. Furthermore, in Chapter 5, you will find detailed insights into the Eightfold Path, which serves as a guide to achieve freedom from suffering. This path encompasses essential aspects such as ethical conduct, mindfulness, and wisdom. By exploring this chapter, you will gain a profound understanding of the transformative steps one can take to attain liberation and cultivate a more harmonious existence.

In Buddhism, Samsara is the continuous cycle of rebirth marked by suffering. To end this cycle, one must attain liberation by overcoming cravings and gaining insight. Rebirth and karma are key concepts in Buddhism. Rebirth explains the differences in wealth and happiness based on past actions. The goal is to achieve liberation by transcending desires and developing wisdom. Karma refers to the idea that actions have consequences, shaping one's future experiences. Positive karma leads to higher realms, while negative karma leads to lower realms. The ultimate objective is to break free from the cycle of rebirth through insight and the cessation of cravings. The upcoming chapter will provide a deeper insight into the concept of karma.

2

THE LAW OF KARMA

IN THE previous chapter, we learned about rebirth and its connection to the law of karma. It is possible that you are curious about whether the law of karma truly exists and how it works. Exploring the concept of karma is important because it offers us a deeper understanding of the cause-and-effect relationship in our existence. It suggests that our actions have consequences, not just in the physical realm but also in the realm of our thoughts, intentions, and emotions. By exploring the concept of karma, we can gain insights into why certain events unfold in our lives and how our actions contribute to those outcomes. Studying karma also helps us reflect on our behavior and choices, taking responsibility for our actions and considering their long-term impact. Understanding karma enables us to make conscious decisions and bring positive change to our lives and others'. It broadens our perspective on life, highlighting how we're all interconnected and how our actions have far-reaching effects. Exploring karma leads to personal growth, self-reflection, and a deeper understanding of the world we live in.

Is Karma Something That Can Be Proven?

Karma is a concept that is difficult to prove or disprove using scientific methods, as it deals with the idea of moral causation and consequences that may transcend our current lifetime. However, Buddhists believe in the concept of karma as a natural law that governs our actions and outcomes. The concept of karma acknowledges that the results of our actions are not always immediately apparent. For example, a person who engages in dishonest behavior may experience temporary success and wealth, but eventually, their actions may catch up to them and lead to negative consequences. Conversely, a person who consistently acts with kindness and compassion may not see immediate rewards, but their actions may have positive ripple effects that are felt over time. In this way, karma suggests that our actions have consequences that may not always be immediately apparent but can influence our lives and the lives of others in significant ways. So, just because we do not see the immediate results of our actions, it does not mean that the concept of karma is not real. Karma exhibits some similarities to the law of effect in that both explain how actions can result in consequences. The law of effect is a fundamental principle in psychology that explains how behaviors are influenced by their consequences. It states that behaviors that are followed by positive consequences, such as rewards or pleasurable outcomes, are more likely to be repeated in the future. On the other hand, behaviors that are followed by negative consequences, such as punishments or unpleasant outcomes, are less likely to be repeated. According to this principle, individuals learn from their experiences and adjust their behaviors accordingly. When a behavior leads to a positive consequence, it creates a sense of satisfaction and reinforces the tendency to engage in that behavior again in similar situations. Positive reinforcement strengthens the association between the behavior and the desired outcome, making it more likely to occur in the future. Conversely, when a behavior leads to a negative consequence, it creates a sense of dissatisfaction or discomfort, discouraging the individual from repeating that behavior. Negative consequences weaken the association between the behavior and the undesirable outcome, reducing the likelihood of engaging in that behavior again. Similarly, karma suggests that our actions can have positive or negative consequences that affect our future experiences. However, while the law of effect is based on observable behavior and reinforcement, karma also takes into account intentions and past actions from past lives in some interpretations. So while the law of effect is concerned with shaping behavior in the present, karma is concerned with the ultimate liberation from suffering.

Dynamics of Actions and Consequences

Many studies have investigated the concept of karma, especially in psychology. Some researchers have looked into how karma beliefs relate to mental well-being, while others have explored how karma beliefs influence behaviors like kindness and helping others.

- One study conducted by **Takashi Kitaoka and colleagues in 2019** examined cultural variations in karma beliefs among individuals from diverse cultural backgrounds. The study aimed to explore how different cultures influence the understanding and interpretation of karma. Participants from various countries, including India, Thailand, Japan, and the United States, took part in the study. They were asked to complete surveys and questionnaires that assessed their beliefs and attitudes toward karma. The findings of the study revealed significant variations in karma beliefs across different cultures. Participants from Eastern cultures, such as India and Thailand, tended to have a stronger belief in karma and its influence on their lives. They perceived karma as a powerful force that governs the consequences of their actions and shapes their present and future experiences. On the other hand, participants from Western cultures, such as the United States, exhibited more diverse beliefs and interpretations of karma. Some saw it as personal responsibility for one's actions, while others viewed it as a broader concept of cause and effect. These cultural differences in karma beliefs highlight the influence of cultural context and upbringing on individuals' understanding and perception of karma. Cultural norms, religious traditions, and philosophical perspectives all contribute to shaping how individuals conceptualize and apply the concept of karma in their lives. Overall, this study highlights the influence of cultural factors on karma beliefs and emphasizes the need to consider cultural context when studying and understanding this concept. It provides valuable insights into how cultural backgrounds shape individuals' perceptions and interpretations of karma.

- A research paper titled **"Karma and Academic Performance" conducted by Ying Wang and colleagues in 2018** examined the relationship between karma beliefs and academic performance in college students. The study likely involved collecting data from college students, measuring their level of belief in karma, and assessing their academic performance using metrics such as GPA or examination scores.

The findings indicated that students who held stronger beliefs in karma tended to have higher levels of academic achievement. This association between karma beliefs and academic performance could potentially be explained by factors such as the students' heightened sense of personal responsibility and their belief in the consequences of their actions. When students perceive a connection between their efforts, actions, and outcomes, influenced by their karma beliefs, they may be more motivated to perform well academically.

- In another study by **Lijun Song and colleagues in 2015**, the relationship between karma beliefs and consumer behavior was examined. The study involved 300 participants from China who completed surveys measuring their karma beliefs and propensity for altruistic behaviors. Participants were asked to rate their agreement with statements related to the concept of karma, such as "I believe that good deeds will be rewarded.". The surveys also included questions about participants' engagement in altruistic behaviors, including volunteering their time and resources and making charitable donations. The results of the study revealed that the relationship between karma beliefs and altruistic behavior was mediated by empathy. In other words, individuals with stronger karma beliefs were more empathetic towards others, which in turn led to a greater propensity for engaging in altruistic acts. This suggests that karma beliefs may foster empathy and concern for others, thereby promoting altruistic behavior. The study also found that karma beliefs were associated with greater life satisfaction and happiness, which is consistent with previous research on the positive effects of religious and spiritual beliefs on well-being. Overall, this study suggests that belief in karma may have a positive impact on behavior and well-being, potentially by promoting empathy and altruistic behavior.

- Another research conducted by **Barbara O'Dair and colleagues in 2011** explored the relationship between karma beliefs and psychological distress. The study included 168 participants, mostly college students, who completed a survey that measured their level of belief in karma along with measures of anxiety, depression, and stress. The results showed that participants who believed in karma reported lower levels of anxiety, depression, and stress than those who did not believe in karma. This suggests that belief in karma may be associated with better psychological well-being. Furthermore, the study found that the relationship between karma beliefs and psychological distress was partially mediated by the participants' level of perceived control over their lives. This means that people who believed in karma also tended to feel more in control of their lives, which in turn was related to lower levels of anxiety, depression, and stress. Overall, the study indicates that believing in karma can potentially benefit mental well-being, possibly because it gives a sense of control and personal responsibility. While karma may not be scientifically verifiable, research suggests that belief in karma can influence one's psychological well-being and behavior. People often draw from personal experiences or observations of others to support the idea that good actions lead to positive outcomes and vice versa. This belief in karma can shape their mindset and actions, as they perceive a connection between their behavior and its consequences. Ultimately, the existence of karma is a matter of personal belief and faith rather than empirical proof.

How Actions Shape Future Lives in Buddhism

In Buddhism, the law of karma plays a central role in understanding the nature of reality. It is a fundamental concept that teaches individuals that they are responsible for their own destiny. According to this law, every action that a person takes, whether it is good or bad, will ultimately affect their future. This means that the consequences of one's actions will be reflected in their future lives and that individuals are responsible for their own destiny. Karma is seen as a force that shapes the world and influences the lives of all beings. The Buddha taught that individuals create their own karma through their thoughts, words, and actions and that this karma determines the quality of their lives. The effects of life are therefore a direct result of one's karma. If a person leads a virtuous life, they will create good karma, which will lead to positive outcomes in their future lives. This may include good health, wealth, and happiness. Conversely, if a person leads an unvirtuous life, they will create bad karma, which will lead to negative outcomes in their future lives. This may include illness, poverty, and suffering. Buddhism teaches that we have the ability to change our karma by changing how we think, speak, and act. By living virtuously and practicing meditation and mindfulness, we can purify our minds and create positive karma. This has the potential to bring greater happiness and fulfillment, both in the present and in the future. Let's dive into the fascinating world of good karma and bad karma, where our actions have the power to shape our destiny and touch our very souls.

Good karma is the accumulation of positive actions and intentions, which can result in good fortune, happiness, and a better future. When we do good deeds, we create positive energy that can benefit us and those around us. Good karma is often associated with the idea that "what goes around, comes around"—when we do good things, good things will come back to us. The benefits of good karma are many. When we act with kindness and generosity, we create a positive atmosphere around us, which can lead to more fulfilling relationships and a greater sense of community. We may also find that our actions are reciprocated, as people are more likely to be kind and helpful to us in return. In addition, good karma can also improve our mental and emotional well-being. When we act with compassion and selflessness, we feel a sense of satisfaction and purpose, which can contribute to a greater sense of happiness and fulfillment. It's important to note that good karma is not just about performing acts of charity or kindness. It also involves cultivating positive attitudes and intentions in our daily lives. For example, if we approach challenges with a positive mindset and a desire to learn and grow, we may find that our efforts are rewarded with success and progress.

Bad karma is the concept that our negative actions and intentions will have negative consequences in the future. It is the accumulation of negative energy resulting from harmful deeds or thoughts. The concept of bad karma is rooted in Buddhism, and it is believed that our actions in this life will have repercussions in the next. When we act with negative intentions or perform harmful actions, we create negative energy that can lead to negative consequences in the future. This negative energy can manifest itself in various forms, such as disease, misfortune, or bad luck. Just as good karma is associated with "what goes around, comes around", bad karma is also associated with this idea. The consequences of bad karma can be many. For example, if we harm others, we may find ourselves experiencing harm in the future. Similarly, if we act with greed or selfishness, we may find ourselves facing financial difficulties or other negative consequences. In addition to the external consequences, bad karma can also have negative effects on our mental and emotional well-being. When we act with negative intentions or perform harmful actions, we create a sense of guilt and regret, which can lead to anxiety, depression, and other mental health issues. It is important to note that bad karma is not a punishment or a form of divine retribution. It is simply the natural consequence of our actions and intentions. However, it is never too late to change our behavior and cultivate positive energy to counteract negative karma.

Karma is often described as a cosmic balance sheet, where every action we take is recorded and tallied over time. Positive actions generate positive karma, while negative actions generate negative karma. This accumulated karma determines our future experiences, both in this life and in potential future lives for those who believe in rebirth. For instance, when someone shows kindness to others, they are believed to accumulate positive karma, which can lead to experiences of happiness, success, and good fortune down the line. Conversely, unethical behavior is thought to generate negative karma, potentially resulting in future experiences of suffering, misfortune, and hardship. I have some true stories about karma that I would like to share.

- One true story of **bad karma** occurred in a small village in Thailand. There was a wealthy man known for his arrogance and disdain for others. He treated his employees poorly, paying them very little and expecting them to work long hours without complaining. Among his employees was a diligent and hardworking young woman who always strived to do her best. Despite her efforts, the man subjected her to mistreatment, assigning her more work than others and showing her no kindness. However, the young woman persevered and remained dedicated to her work, displaying unwavering kindness in the face of adversity. Her resilience and admirable character caught the attention of the man's son, who was captivated by her inner beauty. Deeply in love, the couple defied the man's disapproval and chose to marry, standing up for their love and commitment. Meanwhile, the wealthy man's fortunes took a downturn. His business failed, and he lost his wealth. Consumed by bitterness, he blamed others for his misfortunes. In contrast, the young woman and her husband thrived, surrounded by love and respect from their community. Eventually, the wealthy man passed away alone and miserable, while the couple enjoyed a fulfilling and prosperous life. This story teaches us the importance of treating others with respect and compassion. The choices we make can shape our destiny, and kindness can lead to a rewarding life.

- Another true story that illustrates the negative effects of **bad karma** caused by taking lives involves a lawyer in Thailand who, when he was young, had many fish of various sizes in his pond. The larger fish would prey on the smaller fish, which was a natural part of their life cycle. The young man enjoyed watching the predator fish chase their prey but became bored when some of the larger fish couldn't catch the smaller ones. He began to search for ways to slow down the small fish so they would be easier targets for the larger fish. First, he cut the fins of the small fish, but they were still able to swim fast. So he tried a different method by taking the fish out of the water and hitting them on their heads with a rubber band. This time, the fish were dizzy and couldn't swim effectively, allowing the larger fish to catch and eat them. As he grew up and pursued a career in law, he suffered from constant headaches and dizziness, similar to seasickness. On one occasion, his illness caused him to make a costly mistake in a case, and he felt regretful that he couldn't perform his job effectively. He sought medical attention, trying different remedies in the hopes of a cure, but nothing worked. The doctors were unable to diagnose the cause of his illness. Eventually, he had to leave his job and take a position at a government organization. One day at work, he found a book left behind. As he flipped through the book, he turned to a page that stated, "Those who harm fish accumulate bad karma and may suffer from brain illnesses." It dawned on him that his interference with the fish's natural life cycle had unknowingly burdened him with the karmic repercussions of their suffering. Feeling remorse for the harm he caused the fish, he sought redemption through prayers and mercy. Miraculously, his illness vanished. It's unbelievable. This story serves as a powerful reminder of the impact of negative karma. Despite his ignorance of the harm he was inflicting on the fish, the lawyer suffered the consequences of his actions. His sudden illness is a poignant reminder that there are consequences for harming or taking the lives of others, even if they are animals. Justice will ultimately prevail.

- There is another story of **bad karma** involving a powerful politician. Despite holding a position of power and influence, he used his authority to commit sexual misconduct with his subordinates and vulnerable individuals, betraying their trust and causing harm. Despite his wrongdoing, he managed to hide behind a respectable façade, using his connections and influence to silence his victims. His predatory behavior caused immense suffering and psychological trauma for those he exploited. However, karma caught up with him when his victims found the courage to speak out, exposing his abusive actions to the nation. The revelations led to public outrage, demanding his resignation and legal action. His political career came crashing down, and he became a symbol of disgrace and shame. Not only did he face professional consequences, but his personal life also fell apart. His family distanced themselves from him, and he became isolated from society. Legal investigations were launched, ensuring he faced accountability for his misconduct. This story serves as a powerful reminder that no one is above the law and that engaging in sexual misconduct and abusing positions of power can have devastating consequences. It underscores the importance of maintaining ethical behavior and respecting the rights and dignity of others.
- One true story of **good karma** is that of a man named Patrick Hutchinson. Hutchinson is a personal trainer and father of four from London, England, who became a viral sensation in 2020 after he was photographed carrying a counter-protester to safety

during a Black Lives Matter demonstration. The incident took place in June 2020 during a protest in London's Trafalgar Square. Hutchinson and his friends noticed a counter-protester who had been beaten and was in danger of being further attacked by the crowd. Without hesitation, Hutchinson and his friends surrounded the man and carried him to safety, protecting him from harm. The act of kindness and bravery was captured on camera and quickly went viral, with many people praising Hutchinson for his selflessness and compassion. Hutchinson later gave interviews in which he explained that he had acted out of a sense of duty to protect others, regardless of their political views or backgrounds. The story of Patrick Hutchinson is a heartwarming example of good karma. His willingness to help a stranger in need, despite the potential danger to himself, is a testament to the power of kindness and empathy. By acting with compassion and respect towards others, we can create a more positive and harmonious world where good deeds are rewarded with good karma.

• Another true story of **good karma** that happened in Asia is the story of Narayanan Krishnan, a social worker from India who founded the Akshaya Trust, an organization that feeds and provides healthcare for homeless people and other vulnerable individuals. Krishnan was a successful chef who worked for a five-star hotel in Switzerland before he returned to his home in India in 2002. One day, he was walking near a temple in the city of Madurai when he saw an elderly man eating his own excrement out of hunger. This moment was a turning point for Krishnan, who decided to dedicate his life to helping those in need.

Since then, Krishnan has been providing free meals to thousands of homeless and destitute individuals every day through the Akshaya Trust. He also provides healthcare services, shelter, and education to help people escape poverty and regain their dignity. Krishnan's work has been recognized internationally, and he has received numerous awards for his selfless service, including the CNN Heroes award in 2010. He continues to inspire others with his compassion and dedication to making the world a better place. The story of Narayanan Krishnan is a powerful example of good karma in Asia. By responding to a moment of crisis with kindness and empathy, Krishnan was able to transform the lives of countless people and bring hope and healing to those who had been marginalized and forgotten. His legacy serves as a reminder of the power of individual action to create positive change and make a difference in the world.

Karma is a concept that offers a lens to understand the world's dynamics and our role within them. It emphasizes the importance of ethical conduct, interconnectedness, and personal accountability. While belief in karma varies, treating others with kindness, compassion, and respect remains vital for personal happiness and the well-being of society. In Buddhism, karma can be purified through meditation, ethical behavior, and wisdom. It reflects the impermanence and interdependence of all phenomena. Positive actions result in favorable outcomes, while negative actions lead to unfavorable consequences. This principle aligns with the concept of cause and effect. Both karma and the principle of causality highlight the impact of our actions and their consequences on our experiences. They share similarities across various fields like physics, chemistry, and biology. For instance, the conservation of energy in physics dictates that energy cannot be created or destroyed, only transformed. In biology, genetic mutations arising from changes in DNA influence an organism's traits and contribute to the evolution of new species over time. Although karma is not scientifically proven, it reminds us that our choices have an impact and encourages responsible behavior. By acknowledging the ripple effect of our actions, we can actively pursue a more compassionate and harmonious existence. The underlying principle of karma resonates with our understanding of cause and effect, serving as a reminder to be mindful of the choices we make.

As you delve into the concept of the cycle of rebirth and karma, you'll encounter the inherent presence of suffering within this cycle. This suffering encompasses not only the mind but also the physical body. However, there is a path to liberation from this suffering. Exploring the concept of non-self becomes crucial in this journey. It teaches us that there is no permanent, unchanging self or soul. Instead, our sense of self is ever-changing and impermanent, shaped by various mental and physical factors. By realizing the true nature of non-self, we can release our attachments and find liberation from the suffering of Samsara. The upcoming chapter will provide a deeper exploration of the concept of non-self.

3

THE CONCEPT OF NON-SELF

I N THE previous chapters, we discovered that our actions have consequences, which is known as karma. We also explored how our attachments to things, people, and outcomes can make us suffer. Now, in this chapter, we will delve deeper into the concept of non-self. By exploring the idea of non-self, we can gain a fresh perspective that empowers us to let go of our attachments. This shift in perception can help alleviate the suffering that arises from clinging and grasping onto things. Through the lens of non-self, we will untangle the complex layers of identification, possessiveness, and craving that contribute to our suffering. By doing so, we can cultivate a greater sense of freedom, liberation, and inner peace in our lives.

Attachment in Buddhist Philosophy

In Buddhism, the idea of attachment is based on the false belief that happiness can be found externally, through material possessions, relationships, status, or even ideas and beliefs.

This misguided belief can result in an unyielding attachment to external objects, people, or circumstances. As a result, when these external entities inevitably undergo changes or are lost, it leads to immense emotional pain and suffering. In this chapter, we will delve deeper into the concept of attachment, exploring its various forms, such as attachment to material possessions, relationships, beliefs, and status. We will further examine how the non-self concept can be incorporated into our lives as a means of reducing attachment and attaining a state of inner peace, ultimately leading to less suffering. By understanding and applying these principles, we can learn to let go of our attachments and find true happiness and contentment within ourselves.

As previously mentioned, attachment can manifest in different forms. It can arise from the ego, which is our sense of self and desires. The ego seeks validation, fulfillment, and a sense of superiority, and it often attaches itself to external objects or outcomes to fulfill these desires. When our attachments stem from the ego, they are driven by a deep-rooted belief that our happiness and self-worth are dependent on possessing or achieving certain things. For example, a person may become attached to material possessions because they symbolize success or enhance their self-image. Similarly, a person may become attached to relationships, expecting them to provide them with love, validation, or a sense of security. Attachments to status or social recognition can also arise from the ego's need for validation and a desire to feel superior or important. These attachments can often be tied to a person's sense of self or ego, as they see these things as integral to their identity or happiness. Recognizing the role of the ego in attachment helps us question its true value. Letting go of attachment and reducing the ego's influence involves self-awareness and mindfulness. It brings freedom, inner peace, and authenticity as we find contentment within ourselves instead of relying on external factors. It requires reflection, self-compassion, and letting go of ego-driven desires and beliefs. By transcending attachment and the ego, we lead a more fulfilling life. Buddhist teachings emphasize the impermanence and insubstantiality of the ego, which can help break down these attachments and lead to a greater understanding of the non-self concept. In this section, we will further explore each of these forms of attachment to gain a better understanding of how they contribute to our suffering.

One common form of attachment is **attachment to material possessions**. This form of attachment is characterized by an insatiable desire to acquire and hold onto physical objects such as money, clothes, gadgets, and other luxury items. Though possessing material things is not necessarily bad, attachment to them can lead to suffering. Such attachment can give rise to feelings of greed, envy, and possessiveness, leading to a constant craving for more things and an inability to appreciate what one already has. Imagine having a vast collection of luxury watches and being unable to resist purchasing a new one every time a new model is released. You spend most of your income on these watches and cannot bear the thought of parting with any of them, even if you rarely wear them. However, if you were to lose your job and could no longer afford them, would you feel upset or suffer due to not being able to buy new watches?

Another form of attachment is **attachment to relationships**. This attachment can manifest in different ways, such as an intense desire to be with a particular person, a fear of being alone, or an inability to let go of past relationships. Such attachment can result in a range of negative emotions, including jealousy, possessiveness, and even anger. It can also lead to the manipulation of others in order to maintain the attachment. Have you ever observed someone who exhibits a strong attachment to their romantic partner? Oftentimes, they may become possessive or jealous if their partner spends time with others, leading to tensions and conflicts within the relationship.

Attachment to status is another common form of attachment. This attachment can manifest as a constant need for validation, comparison with others, and the belief that one's worth is determined by their position or wealth. When this attachment is not fulfilled or is threatened, it can lead to feelings of inadequacy, anxiety, and disappointment. When I was in school, I observed some friends who were overly attached to their academic achievements and the status that comes with being at the top of the class. They may become obsessed with getting perfect grades, even if it means sacrificing their mental health and well-being. They may also be competitive with their peers and become upset if they feel someone else is outperforming them. I once had a friend who excelled academically throughout high school, but when he started studying engineering in college, his GPA noticeably declined. There were various reasons for this, but a significant factor was his tendency to compare his performance with that of his old high school friends, many of whom were still maintaining good grades. This constant comparison likely led to feelings of depression and inadequacy. Sadly, in his last year of college, he took his own life. The loss of my friend was devastating, and his family and friends will forever miss him.

Lastly, *attachment to ideas and beliefs* can also lead to suffering. This attachment is characterized by a rigid adherence to particular beliefs or ideas, often to the point of ignoring evidence that contradicts them. Such attachment can result in a closed-minded approach to life and can lead to conflict

THE BUDDHA SAID WHAT?!

with others who hold different beliefs or ideas. For example, people can become very attached to their political beliefs and affiliations, often to the point where they are unwilling to consider alternative viewpoints or compromise with those who hold different beliefs.

By understanding the different forms of attachment, we can become more aware of how they manifest in our own lives and take steps to reduce their hold on us. Incorporating the non-self concept can help us to loosen our attachment to external things and focus instead on finding happiness within ourselves. In Buddhism, the practice of non-attachment, or letting go, is considered to be the key to reducing attachment and the suffering it causes. This is achieved through mindfulness and detachment. Mindfulness entails being fully present and aware of our thoughts, emotions, and sensations without any judgment or attachment to them. On the other hand, detachment involves recognizing the impermanence of all things and letting go of our attachment to them. By engaging in mindfulness and detachment practices, we can develop a deeper sense of inner peace and joy that is not influenced by external circumstances. We can liberate ourselves from the cycle of suffering by relinquishing our attachments to things and people and discovering a greater sense of fulfillment in the present moment.

The Dance of Ego and Non-Self

As previously mentioned, attachment can arise from the ego, and the idea of the non-self plays a crucial role in diminishing its influence. In Buddhist philosophy, the ego (Atta) and non-self (Anatta) concepts are crucial for understanding the nature of self and reality. They help reduce attachment and lead to liberation. Let's explore the ego and non-self concepts in greater detail, delving into their intricacies and implications.

The Ego or Atta, is a concept that refers to the sense of self, or the belief that we are separate and distinct individuals with our own unique identity, personality, and experience. The ego is deeply ingrained in our culture and society and is often seen as an essential part of our being. It arises from our identification with our thoughts, emotions, and possessions. We become attached to these things and develop a sense of ownership over them. When we don't get what we want or lose something we are attached to, we feel a sense of loss, frustration, and even anger. These negative emotions create suffering, which is perpetuated by our attachment to the ego. The idea of karma is closely tied to the concept of ego. It suggests that our actions have consequences that shape our present and future experiences. Our ego, or sense of self, significantly influences our intentions and behaviors, resulting in karmic imprints that shape our future outcomes. Acting from a place of ego and self-interest often leads to negative karma and subsequent suffering. On the other hand, acting with compassion and recognizing our interconnectedness with others generates positive karma, resulting in a profound sense of fulfillment. In Buddhism, the ego is seen as an illusion that brings about suffering. Believing in a permanent and unchanging self is considered the root cause of our suffering. This belief leads to attachment, craving, and aversion, perpetuating a cycle of suffering. By being mindful and aware of our ego, we can become more conscious of our actions and create positive karma that benefits ourselves and others. Non-attachment, or letting go of the ego, is a key practice to alleviate suffering. Letting go of our attachment to the ego allows us to recognize that it is a mental construct and not our true self. Embracing mindfulness and detachment allows us to remain present, free from judgment and attachment, fostering inner peace and lasting happiness that are independent of external circumstances.

Non-self or Anatta, on the other hand, asserts the non-existence of a permanent and independent self or soul. According to Buddhist teachings, everything in the universe is in a constant state of flux and change, and there is no fixed or unchanging essence that exists independently of everything else. This includes ourselves; our thoughts, emotions, and physical form are constantly changing, and there is no underlying substance that persists over time. The sense of self that we experience is a product of our thoughts, perceptions, and experiences, and it is not a fixed or permanent reality. By recognizing this, we can let go of our attachment to the self and cultivate a deeper sense of inner peace and freedom from suffering. To understand non-self, it is indeed helpful to have knowledge of the five aggregates of self. According to Buddhist teachings, the five aggregates are the components that together create the illusion of a separate and enduring self. These aggregates include form (the physical body), feelings, perceptions, mental formations (thoughts and emotions), and consciousness. By recognizing that these aggregates are impermanent and constantly changing, we can realize the absence of a fixed and independent self. Comprehending the five aggregates is crucial to understanding non-self, and having a clear understanding of the essential aspects of non-self is key to releasing our attachments. These aspects are fundamental concepts in Buddhist philosophy that challenge our conventional understanding of selfhood. They can be summarized as follows:

- **Impermanence:** This aspect emphasizes the impermanent and ever-changing nature of all phenomena, including ourselves. Everything in the world undergoes a cycle of arising, existing for a period, and eventually ceasing to exist. Our bodies, thoughts, emotions, and experiences are all subject to this impermanence. Often, we hold onto things that we believe will bring us happiness or security, such as relationships, possessions, or achievements. However, when we realize that everything is impermanent and bound to change, we can let go of our attachment to these things and find contentment in the present moment. By acknowledging impermanence, we release the illusion of a fixed and unchanging self. For instance, if we recognize that a challenging relationship is causing us suffering but persist in holding onto it out of fear of being alone, understanding impermanence can give us the strength to let go of this attachment. In doing so, we open ourselves up to greater happiness and inner peace.

• **Interdependence:** This aspect underscores the interconnectedness of all phenomena. According to Buddhist teachings, nothing exists in isolation; everything is interconnected and dependent on various causes and conditions. This realization helps us understand that there is no independent, separate self that exists apart from the rest of existence. While we may perceive ourselves as separate beings, the truth is that we are intricately interconnected with the world around us. This interconnectedness extends to all aspects of our existence, including our thoughts, emotions, and experiences. By recognizing this interconnected nature, we can let go of the illusion of separateness and cultivate a sense of unity and compassion. For example, when we acknowledge that our actions affect not only ourselves but also others and the environment, we become more mindful of the consequences of our choices. We understand that our well-being is intertwined with the well-being of others and the world. This awareness inspires us to act with greater responsibility and consideration for the interconnected web of life. By embracing this interconnected view, we shift our perspective from self-centeredness to a broader sense of connection and interdependence. We develop a deeper appreciation for the intricate relationships and interplay of all phenomena, finding meaning and purpose in our interconnected existence.

- **Lack of Control:** This aspect challenges the notion of ultimate control over ourselves and external circumstances. Despite our desires and efforts to manipulate and control life, many aspects remain beyond our grasp. Our thoughts, emotions, and even our bodies are influenced by numerous causes and conditions that are beyond our control. By recognizing the limitations of control, we cultivate a sense of acceptance and surrender to the natural flow of life. Often, we strongly identify with our possessions, achievements, and our concept of self. However, when we understand that there is no fixed self that possesses or controls anything, we can release our attachment to these things and discover greater freedom and ease. For instance, we might realize that our sense of identity is tied to our career or societal status, leading us to feel lost or anxious when facing setbacks or failures. By letting go of the illusion of control, we cultivate acceptance and surrender to the natural flow of life.

- **Not-self Nature:** This aspect reveals that the self we perceive is not an inherent or independent entity. Instead, it is a composite of ever-changing elements. Our thoughts, feelings, sensations, and perceptions arise and fade away, giving the illusion of a continuous and fixed self. However, upon closer examination, we discover that there is no solid and unchanging essence defining who we are. The non-self nature is a fundamental aspect of reality, indicating that there is no essential and enduring "I" or "me" throughout our lives. Recognizing the non-self nature helps us release the grip of attachment and the illusion of a fixed identity. It teaches us that our experiences and the world are in constant flux. We understand that we are not separate from the world but intricately connected to it. This understanding opens the door to a more expansive and compassionate perspective. We become aware of the interconnectedness of all beings and the impact our actions and choices have on others and the world. Practicing mindfulness and insight meditation are ways to cultivate a direct and experiential understanding of the non-self nature. Through these practices, we observe the impermanence and interdependence of our thoughts, feelings, and sensations. Gradually, we loosen our identification with them and awaken to a more liberated and awakened way of being. By embracing the non-self nature, we can experience greater freedom, compassion, and wisdom. We let go of the illusion of a fixed self, opening ourselves to the dynamic flow of life. This understanding deepens our capacity for empathy and interconnectedness, fostering a sense of unity and harmony with all existence.

Understanding these essential aspects of non-self challenges our deeply ingrained sense of a separate and enduring self. It invites us to question our attachments, cravings, and identifications with temporary phenomena. By realizing the impermanence, interdependence, lack of control, and not-self nature of our experience, we can gradually release our attachments and reduce suffering. This profound shift in perspective opens the path to liberation and a deeper sense of interconnectedness with all beings and phenomena. Overall, the concept of non-self teaches us to let go of our attachment to the idea of a fixed and independent self and to recognize the impermanent and interdependent nature of all phenomena. By doing so, we can reduce our attachment to material possessions, relationships, and even our own sense of self. As a result, we can alleviate suffering, find inner peace, and attain liberation. Letting go involves accepting the present moment, questioning our attachments, defining ourselves with flexibility, releasing attachment to the past, introspecting, and recognizing that attachment disrupts our peace of mind and self-control. By applying these techniques, we can reduce attachment to people, objects, and ideas, thereby experiencing greater inner peace and happiness. Ultimately, detachment is viewed as a crucial path to enlightenment.

Letting Go of Ego

As mentioned earlier, ego is considered one of the main obstacles on the path to enlightenment. One way to reduce ego is to cultivate the practice of mindfulness. By becoming more aware of our thoughts, feelings, and actions, we can start to recognize when our ego is in control and begin to let go of it. This can be done through meditation and other mindfulness practices, such as paying attention to our breathing or focusing on the present moment, which we will learn in the following chapters. Another way to reduce ego is to develop compassion and empathy for others. By recognizing the interconnectedness of all beings, we can begin to let go of the idea that we are separate and special. This can be done through practices such as loving-kindness meditation, where we send positive thoughts and feelings to ourselves and others. Buddhism also emphasizes the importance of letting go of attachments and desires. This means recognizing that our ego-driven desires are often the source of our suffering. By letting go of these desires, we can free ourselves from the cycle of craving and aversion that perpetuates our sense of self-importance. Finally, Buddhism teaches the importance of cultivating humility. This means recognizing that we are not inherently special or better than anyone else. By letting go of our sense of superiority or inferiority, we can begin to see ourselves and others more clearly without the distortion of ego. To reduce ego, Buddhism emphasizes mindfulness, compassion, detachment, and humility. These practices help us move towards enlightenment by loosening the grip of the ego. Reducing attachment is also essential for inner peace and happiness.

Here are some steps to **reduce attachments**:

1. Practice letting things be and releasing the need to control everything.
2. Question your attachment to people, things, and circumstances.
3. Accept the present moment for what it is, without grasping, owning, or controlling it.
4. Define yourself in fluid terms, hold relationships lightly, interact with many people, and do not fear the future.
5. Let go of attachment to the past, forgive yourself, and focus on present love rather than fear.

THE BUDDHA SAID WHAT?!

6. Look within yourself and learn to love yourself, which can help reduce attachment to others.

It's important to keep in mind that attachment can lead to a loss of inner peace and self-control and that it's crucial to avoid overemphasizing the positive qualities of others. Through practicing these steps, one can decrease attachment and attain a greater sense of peace and happiness in life. Reducing attachment to the concept of atta or ego is a gradual process that requires continuous practice. By cultivating these qualities, we can slowly reduce our attachment to the idea of a permanent self or soul and develop a deeper understanding of the nature of reality.

As discussed earlier in the previous chapters, one of the principal causes of suffering is the absence of comprehension of the Four Noble Truths. We have also come to the realization that the Noble Eightfold Path, which is an essential part of the Fourth Noble Truth, is the way to minimize attachment and alleviate suffering. In the next two chapters, we will delve into the details of both the Four Noble Truths and the Noble Eightfold Path.

4

THE FOUR NOBLE TRUTHS

A S YOU have learned in the previous chapter, the Four Noble Truths are considered one of the most important and fundamental teachings in Buddhism. They provide a framework for understanding the nature of suffering and the path to liberation from it. The Four Noble Truths continue to be studied and practiced by millions of Buddhists around the world, as well as by people of other faiths and philosophies who find value in their teachings. We can adapt the Four Noble Truths into our daily lives by incorporating the teachings and principles into our thoughts, words, and actions. By doing so, we can develop a deeper understanding of ourselves, others, and the world around us. We can learn to transform our suffering into opportunities for growth and cultivate greater peace, happiness, and fulfillment in our lives. This chapter aims to provide a comprehensive understanding of the Four Noble Truths, which can be applied in everyday life to reduce suffering and achieve greater peace. It is my hope that this knowledge will be beneficial to all who study and apply it.

Exploring the Essence of the Four Noble Truths

The Four Noble Truths are a fundamental teaching of Buddhism that outlines the path to liberation from suffering. The Buddha, after years of spiritual practice and self-inquiry, first articulated these truths upon attaining enlightenment. Before his enlightenment, he had lived a life of luxury as a prince, but he became disillusioned with the world and set out on a quest to discover the nature of suffering and how to overcome it. The first noble truth arose within him as he recognized the inherent suffering in life. The second noble truth emerged when he understood that craving and attachment are the causes of suffering. The third noble truth was revealed when he realized that suffering can be overcome through the cessation of craving and attachment. Lastly, the fourth noble truth dawned upon him as he comprehended the Noble Eightfold Path, the path leading to the cessation of suffering. The Buddha's insights into the nature of suffering and the path to liberation were revolutionary for his time and continue to be a powerful source of inspiration and guidance for Buddhists around the world. The Buddha first taught these truths during his first sermon after achieving enlightenment, and they remain a central part of Buddhist philosophy and practice. If we delve deeper into each of the noble truths, we can gain a more profound understanding of their essence. Shall we explore each truth in greater detail and discuss them further?

The First Noble Truth: The Truth of Suffering, or Dukkha, also known as "suffering", is the first noble truth, which refers to the inherent unsatisfactory nature of life and the pervasive sense of dissatisfaction that arises from our experiences. It encompasses not only the obvious forms of suffering, such as physical pain or emotional distress, but also the subtle forms of dissatisfaction that arise from clinging, craving, and attachment. It is directly related to the Five Aggregates which are the five components of human existence that give rise to this suffering. These include form, sensation or feeling, perception, mental formations, and consciousness. The Five Aggregates are considered impermanent and constantly changing, and it is the attachment and clinging to these aggregates that lead to suffering. For example, an individual may experience physical pain or discomfort (form), and this may lead to negative emotions and thoughts (mental formations) such as anger or frustration. These negative mental formations then lead to further suffering, as the individual may cling to these feelings and experiences and resist the impermanent nature of the physical pain. Dukkha is an unavoidable part of human existence. It arises from the impermanence and changing nature of life. No matter how much we try to seek happiness and avoid suffering, we are bound to encounter difficulties, loss, and the inevitable changes that life brings. It can manifest in various ways, such as the pain of loss, the frustration of unfulfilled desires, the anxiety of uncertainty, or the dissatisfaction with imperfection. Dukkha is a core concept in Buddhism, and it encompasses a broader range of negative emotions and experiences. In real life, there are many examples of dukkha that people may experience. Here are some:

- **Illness:** When people fall ill, they often experience physical discomfort, pain, and emotional distress. They may be unable to do the things they normally enjoy or be unable to work, which can lead to feelings of frustration and helplessness.
- **Loss:** Whether it is the death of a loved one, the end of a relationship, or the loss of a job, people often experience grief and sadness in response to loss.

These emotions can be intense and long-lasting, and they can disrupt people's lives and sense of well-being.

- **Aging:** As people age, they may experience physical and cognitive decline, which can limit their ability to do things they once enjoyed. They may also face new challenges, such as social isolation, financial insecurity, or health problems, which can lead to feelings of anxiety and uncertainty.
- **Daily Stress:** Even in the absence of major life events, people may experience stress and dissatisfaction as they navigate the challenges of daily life. They may feel overwhelmed by work, family obligations, or other responsibilities, or they may struggle with feelings of boredom or ennui.

These are just a few examples of the many forms of dukkha that people may encounter in their lives. The Buddha taught that dukkha is an inevitable part of human existence. Recognizing the reality of dukkha is the first step towards understanding and addressing it. By acknowledging the presence of suffering in our lives, we can develop a deeper sense of empathy and compassion for ourselves and others. It also motivates us to seek liberation from suffering and find a path towards lasting happiness and inner peace. To let go of attachment and reduce suffering, it is crucial to understand the impermanence, unsatisfactoriness, and absence of a fixed self or essence (non-self), as we have learned in the previous chapter. Developing mindfulness and awareness of the present moment is key. By recognizing the impermanence of all things and the interconnectedness of phenomena, we can let go of attachment to specific experiences or sensations. Our perceptions and experiences of the sense doors (such as sight, sound, smell, taste, touch, thoughts, and emotions) and sense objects shape our attachments. Understanding the role of sense doors and sense objects is crucial to navigating attachment and finding greater freedom. Additionally, we can practice letting go of attachment by following these steps:

- **Awareness:** The first step is to be aware of our attachment to sense objects through the sense doors. We can do this by observing our thoughts and feelings when we come into contact with sense objects.
- **Mindfulness:** Once we are aware of our attachment, we can practice mindfulness to stay present in the moment and observe our thoughts and feelings without judgment.
- **Investigation:** We can investigate our attachment to sense objects by asking ourselves why we are attached to them and what benefit we gain from holding onto them.
- **Reflection:** Reflection involves reflecting on the impermanence and unsatisfactoriness of sense objects. By recognizing that sense objects are impermanent and constantly changing, we can begin to let go of our attachment to them.
- **Practice:** Finally, we can practice letting go of attachment by consciously choosing to redirect our attention away from sense objects and towards more wholesome thoughts and actions. This involves cultivating positive habits and focusing on activities that bring us genuine happiness and contentment, rather than temporary pleasures.

The Buddha taught that the way to overcome suffering is not by seeking pleasure or avoiding pain but by developing an understanding of the true nature of reality and the impermanence of all things. By accepting the truth of suffering, we can begin to let go of our attachment to things that are impermanent and find lasting peace and happiness on the path to enlightenment. By following these steps, we can gradually let go of our attachment to sense objects and reduce our suffering. Practicing meditation and contemplation can also help cultivate this awareness and develop the ability to observe our thoughts and feelings without becoming attached to them. It is also important to recognize the role of craving and attachment in our suffering and to cultivate a sense of contentment and equanimity in our daily lives. Additionally, developing compassion and loving-kindness towards oneself and others can help reduce attachment and cultivate a greater sense of connectedness and empathy towards all beings. Through these practices, one can gradually let go of attachment and experience a greater sense of peace and contentment in life. The interconnectedness of these teachings suggests that recognizing the impermanent nature of our experiences and the role that our attachment and aversion play in causing suffering is key to understanding the First Noble Truth. By developing mindfulness and awareness of our experiences through the lens of the Five Aggregates and the Sense Doors and Sense Objects, we can begin to see our experiences more clearly and find a path to liberation from suffering. Overall, the interconnection between the First Noble Truth, the Five Aggregates, and the concepts of Sense Doors and Sense Objects provides a comprehensive framework for understanding the nature of suffering. By cultivating mindfulness and awareness, we can begin to break free from the cycle of suffering and find greater peace and contentment in the present moment.

The Second Noble Truth: The Origin of Suffering, also known as Samudaya, is the second of the Four Noble Truths, and it refers to the origin or cause of suffering. According to the Buddha, the cause of suffering is craving or attachment, which arises from ignorance of the true nature of reality, particularly the craving for pleasure, material possessions, and ego-gratification. We refuse to accept life as it is. The more we cling to these things, the more we suffer when they are taken away or fail to satisfy us. In real life, there are many examples of how craving and attachment can lead to suffering. Here are some:

- **Material possessions:** People often crave material possessions such as expensive cars, clothes, or gadgets. They may feel that these objects will bring them happiness or make them more desirable to others. However, when they are unable to obtain these possessions or lose them, they may experience feelings of disappointment, frustration, or even despair.

- **Relationships:** People may become attached to others, such as romantic partners, family members, or friends. They may feel that these relationships define who they are or provide them with a sense of security and belonging. However, when these relationships end or change, they may experience feelings of grief, loneliness, or even anger.

- **Power and status:** People may crave power, status, or recognition from others. They may feel that these things will give them a sense of control or importance. However, when they are unable to obtain these things or lose them, they may experience feelings of worthlessness or insecurity.

- **Pleasure:** People may become attached to pleasure in the form of food, drugs, sex, or other sensory experiences. They may feel that these experiences provide them with a sense of happiness or an escape from their problems. However, when they are unable to obtain these experiences or when they become addicted to them, they may experience feelings of emptiness, addiction, or even despair.

These are just a few examples of how craving and attachment can lead to suffering in real life. The Buddha taught that the way to overcome suffering is to cultivate wisdom, ethical conduct, and mindfulness, which can help people see through the illusions of craving and attachment and find true peace and happiness.

The Third Noble Truth: The Cessation of Suffering, also known as Nirodha, refers to the state of liberation from suffering and the end of the cycle of birth, death, and rebirth. The Buddha taught that it is possible to overcome suffering by letting go of attachment and craving. When we cultivate mindfulness, wisdom, and compassion, we can break free from the cycle of suffering and achieve a state of peace and contentment. Nirodha is an important concept in Buddhist philosophy. According to the Buddha's teachings, suffering is a fundamental aspect of life, but it is possible to achieve freedom from suffering through the cessation of craving and attachment. In practice, Nirodha is attained by cultivating detachment and non-attachment to alleviate the causes of our suffering. By recognizing that all things are impermanent and ultimately unsatisfactory, we can learn to let go of our attachment to them and find peace in the present moment. One example of Nirodha in real life is when we experience the loss of a loved one. This is a difficult and painful experience, but by accepting the impermanence of life and the inevitability of death, we can find a sense of peace and acceptance in the face of our grief. Another example of Nirodha is when we let go of our attachment to material possessions and status. By recognizing that these things are ultimately unsatisfactory and impermanent, we can find a sense of contentment and fulfillment in the present moment rather than constantly striving for more and never feeling truly satisfied. In addition, the practice of mindfulness meditation can help us achieve Nirodha by developing awareness and acceptance of our present experience. By cultivating a non-judgmental and non-reactive attitude towards our thoughts and emotions, we can learn to let go of our attachment to them and find a sense of peace and equanimity. In conclusion, Nirodha is a powerful concept that can help us find freedom from suffering in our daily lives. By cultivating detachment and non-attachment towards the things that cause us pain and discomfort, we can find peace and contentment in the present moment and live more fulfilling and meaningful lives.

The Fourth Noble Truth: The Path to the Cessation of Suffering, or Magga, also known as the Noble Eightfold Path, is the path to the cessation of suffering in Buddhist philosophy. It is considered one of the central teachings of the Buddha and is seen as a roadmap for achieving enlightenment and liberation from suffering. The Noble Eightfold Path consists of eight interconnected steps or practices, each of which is seen as essential for achieving the ultimate goal of Nirodha, or the cessation of suffering. These eight steps are:

- **Right View:** Having an accurate understanding of the nature of reality, including the nature of suffering, impermanence, and non-self
- **Right Intention:** Cultivating the intention to act with compassion, generosity, and wisdom rather than out of greed, hatred, or delusion
- **Right Speech:** Using our words in a way that is honest, kind, and beneficial and avoiding speech that is harmful, divisive, or untrue

- **Right Action:** Behaving in a way that is ethical, compassionate, and in line with our values and beliefs
- **Right Livelihood:** Making a living in a way that is ethical, does not harm others, and is in line with our values and beliefs
- **Right Effort:** Making a consistent effort to cultivate positive qualities such as compassion, generosity, and wisdom and to overcome negative qualities such as greed, hatred, and delusion
- **Right Mindfulness:** Cultivating a state of awareness and acceptance in the present moment and developing a deeper understanding of our thoughts, emotions, and experiences
- **Right Concentration:** Cultivating the ability to focus our mind and develop a deep and sustained level of concentration, which can lead to states of insight and enlightenment

In order to achieve the ultimate goal of Nirodha, each of these eight steps is seen as essential and interdependent. By practicing each step in a balanced and integrated way, we can gradually reduce our suffering and cultivate a deeper sense of peace and well-being in our lives. The Noble Eightfold Path is a comprehensive and holistic approach to achieving the cessation of suffering in Buddhist philosophy. By cultivating ethical behavior, wisdom, and compassion and by developing mindfulness and concentration, we can gradually overcome the causes of suffering and achieve a state of enlightenment and liberation. In real life, we can apply the principles of the Noble Eightfold Path in a variety of ways to reduce our suffering and increase our sense of well-being. For example, we can practice right speech by being mindful of our words and avoiding speech that is harmful, divisive, or untrue. By speaking in a kind and compassionate manner, we can reduce conflict and promote harmony in our relationships. Similarly, we can practice right action by behaving in a way that is ethical and compassionate. This might involve making choices that benefit others, avoiding harmful behaviors, and living in a way that aligns with our values and beliefs. Right mindfulness is another important aspect of the Noble Eightfold Path, and it involves cultivating a state of awareness and acceptance in the present moment. By practicing mindfulness meditation, we can develop a deeper understanding of our thoughts, emotions, and experiences and learn to relate to them in a more balanced and compassionate way.

The Noble Eightfold Path is a comprehensive and holistic approach to achieving the cessation of suffering in Buddhist philosophy. By cultivating ethical behavior, wisdom, and compassion and by developing mindfulness and concentration, we can gradually overcome the causes of suffering and achieve a state of enlightenment and liberation. Ultimately, the path to the cessation of suffering is a lifelong journey that requires dedication, discipline, and patience. By incorporating the principles of the Noble Eightfold Path into our daily lives, we can gradually reduce our suffering and increase our sense of peace and contentment. In the upcoming chapter, we will delve deeper into The Noble Eightfold Path and explore practical ways of incorporating it into our daily lives.

5

THE NOBLE EIGHTFOLD PATH

A S WE learned in the previous chapter, the Noble Eightfold Path is a roadmap for achieving enlightenment and liberation from suffering. By following this path, we can gradually overcome our attachments and cravings and achieve a state of peace and happiness. This chapter will delve deeper into the path and explore its nuances.

Buddhist Eightfold Path

The Noble Eightfold Path consists of eight interconnected steps that guide us towards a state of enlightenment and liberation from suffering. Each step on the path builds on the one before it, and they are meant to be practiced together in order to achieve the ultimate goal of Nirodha, or the cessation of suffering. It is a set of eight practices or steps that are seen as essential for achieving enlightenment and liberation from suffering. It includes: Right Views (the Four Noble Truths), Right Intention, Right Speech, Right Action, Right Livelihood, Right Effort, Right Mindfulness (total concentration in activity), and Right Concentration (meditation). These eight practices are interconnected and mutually supportive and are meant to be practiced together in order to achieve the ultimate goal of Nirodha, or the cessation of suffering. The principle of the Middle Way is inherent in the Noble Eightfold Path, which reflects the teachings and life of the Buddha. The Middle Way represents a rejection of all extremes of thought, emotion, action, and lifestyle. Rather than either severe mortification of the body or a life of indulgence in insidious pleasures, the Buddha advocated a moderate, or balanced," wandering lifestyle and the cultivation of mental and emotional equanimity through meditation and morality. The Noble Eightfold Path is traditionally divided into three categories: wisdom, ethics, and mental development. These categories reflect the idea that in order to achieve the ultimate goal of Nirodha, we must cultivate wisdom, ethical behavior, and mental discipline.

The first category of the Noble Eightfold Path is **Wisdom**, which includes the first two practices:

1. **Right View** is the first step in the Noble Eightfold Path, which leads to liberation from suffering and the attainment of enlightenment. It refers to having an accurate understanding of the nature of reality, including the nature of suffering, impermanence, and non-self. It is about seeing the world as it truly is, rather than through the distorted lens of our own desires and beliefs. Right View is essential because it provides the foundation for all the other practices on the path. Without a clear understanding of the nature of reality, it is impossible to cultivate wisdom, ethical behavior, and mental discipline. In real life, there are many examples of how the practice of Right View can be applied. For instance, if we are facing a difficult

situation, such as a job loss or the end of a relationship, we may be tempted to see it as a personal failure or a reflection of our inherent inadequacy. However, if we cultivate the Right View, we can see the situation as an impermanent and ever-changing phenomenon that is a natural part of the human experience. We can also see that our own perceptions and beliefs are creating much of the suffering we are experiencing, and we can work to change those beliefs in order to reduce our suffering. Another example of how Right View can be applied is in our relationships with others. If we believe that we are separate and independent individuals with our own needs and desires that are separate from others, we may act in ways that harm others in order to fulfill our own needs. However, if we cultivate the Right View, we can see that all beings are interconnected and interdependent and that our own well-being is intimately connected to the well-being of others. We can develop a sense of empathy and compassion for others and act in ways that benefit everyone, rather than just ourselves.

The practice of Right View is about developing a deeper understanding of the nature of reality and seeing the world with clarity and wisdom. By cultivating this practice, we can reduce our own and others' suffering and move towards a state of enlightenment and liberation. Here are some examples of how Right View can be practiced in daily life.

a. **Seeing The Impermanence of All Things:** By recognizing that all things, including ourselves, are impermanent and subject to change, we can develop a deeper appreciation for the present moment and cultivate a sense of detachment from material possessions.

b. **Recognizing The Interconnectedness of All Beings:** By understanding that all beings are interconnected and interdependent, we can cultivate compassion and empathy for others.

c. **Understanding The Law of Cause and Effect:** By recognizing that our actions have consequences, both in this life and in future lives, we can cultivate a sense of responsibility and ethical behavior

d. **Developing a Sense of Spiritual Inquiry:** By asking questions about the nature of reality and seeking answers through spiritual practices, we can develop a deeper understanding of the world around us and our place in it.

In summary, Right View is about developing an understanding of the Four Noble Truths and the nature of reality. It involves recognizing the impermanence of all things, the interconnectedness of all beings, the law of cause and effect, and developing a sense of spiritual inquiry. By practicing Right View, one can develop a deeper understanding of oneself and the world, leading to greater happiness and well-being.

2. **Right Intention** is the second step of the Noble Eightfold Path. It refers to cultivating intentions that are in alignment with the principles of non-harm, non-ill will, and non-greed. It is about developing a genuine desire to cultivate compassion, generosity, and kindness, and to let go of harmful thoughts and behaviors. In order to practice Right Intention, we must first cultivate awareness of our own thoughts

and intentions. We must recognize when we are motivated by selfish desires or harmful intentions, and make a conscious effort to redirect our thoughts towards more positive and compassionate intentions. In real life, there are many examples of how the practice of Right Intention can be applied. For instance, if we are in a conflict with someone, we may be tempted to respond with anger and resentment, with the intention of hurting the other person. However, if we cultivate Right Intention, we can recognize the harm that such actions would cause, and instead respond with kindness and compassion, with the intention of resolving the conflict in a peaceful and constructive way. Another example of how Right Intention can be applied is in our interactions with others. If we are motivated by the desire for personal gain or recognition, we may act in ways that are harmful to others, such as manipulating or exploiting them for our own benefit. However, if we cultivate Right Intention, we can recognize the harm that such actions would cause, and instead act with generosity and compassion, with the intention of benefiting others as well as ourselves. The practice of Right Intention is about developing a genuine desire to cultivate compassion, generosity, and kindness, and to let go of harmful thoughts and behaviors. By cultivating this practice, we can reduce our own suffering and the suffering of others, and move towards a state of enlightenment and liberation.

In Buddhism, Right Intention is the intention to cultivate wholesome attitudes and actions and to let go of unwholesome attitudes and actions. The Buddha defined Right Intention as the intention to renounce selfish desires and to cultivate compassion and loving-kindness towards all beings. Here are some examples of how Right Intention can be practiced in daily life:

a. **Cultivating Compassion:** By intentionally cultivating compassion towards all beings, one can develop a sense of empathy and understanding for others. This can be done through practices such as metta meditation, which involves sending loving-kindness to oneself and others.

b. **Letting Go of Anger and Ill-will:** By intentionally letting go of anger and ill-will towards others, one can cultivate a sense of inner peace and harmony. This can be done through practices such as forgiveness meditation, which involves letting go of resentment and grudges towards oneself and others.

c. **Practicing Generosity:** By intentionally practicing generosity towards others, one can cultivate a sense of selflessness and altruism. This can be done through acts of kindness, such as volunteering or donating to charity.

d. **Renouncing Harmful Desires:** By intentionally renouncing harmful desires, such as cravings for material possessions or unhealthy relationships, one can cultivate a sense of contentment and inner peace.

In summary, Right Intention is about cultivating wholesome attitudes and actions and letting go of unwholesome attitudes and actions. It involves the intention to renounce selfish desires and cultivate compassion and loving kindness towards all beings. By practicing Right Intention, one can cultivate a deep sense of inner peace and happiness, leading to greater well-being and fulfillment in life.

The second category of the Noble Eightfold Path is **Ethics**, which includes the next three practices:

3. **Right Speech** is the third step of the Noble Eightfold Path. It refers to speaking in ways that are truthful, kind, and beneficial to oneself and others. It is about using your words to promote harmony, understanding, and compassion rather than causing harm or discord. In order to practice Right Speech, we must first cultivate mindfulness and awareness of our own speech. We should be aware of our words and avoid causing harm to others. We must also be mindful of the words we use, making sure they are truthful, clear, and appropriate to the situation. In real life, there are many examples of how the practice of Right Speech can be applied. For instance, if we are engaged in a heated argument with someone, we may be tempted to use harsh and hurtful words with the intention of winning the argument or hurting the other person. However, if we cultivate Right Speech, we can recognize the harm that such words would cause and instead speak in ways that are calm, truthful, and compassionate, with the intention of resolving the conflict in a peaceful and constructive way. Another example of how Right Speech can be applied is in our daily interactions with others. If we gossip or spread rumors about others, we may cause harm to their reputation and relationships, as well as our own. However, if we cultivate Right Speech, we can speak in ways that are truthful, kind, and

respectful and avoid spreading harmful rumors or engaging in gossip.

Overall, the practice of Right Speech is about using our words to promote harmony, understanding, and compassion rather than causing harm or discord. By cultivating this practice, we can reduce our own and others' suffering and move towards a state of enlightenment and liberation. The Buddha defined Right Speech as avoiding lying, gossiping, harsh language, and idle chatter. Instead, one should speak truthfully, avoid hurtful or divisive words, and speak only when necessary and in a way that is beneficial to others. Here are some examples of how Right Speech can be practiced in daily life:

a. **Speaking Truthfully:** By speaking truthfully, one can cultivate a sense of integrity and trustworthiness. This can be done by avoiding exaggeration, distortion, and fabrication of the truth and speaking only what one knows to be true.

b. **Avoiding Gossip and Divisive Speech:** By avoiding gossip and divisive speech, one can cultivate a sense of harmony and goodwill towards others. This can be done by refraining from speaking negatively about others, spreading rumors, or creating division among people.

c. **Using Kind and Gentle Language:** By using kind and gentle language, one can cultivate a sense of compassion and empathy towards others. This can be done by speaking in a tone that is respectful, kind, and considerate and avoiding harsh or aggressive language.

THE BUDDHA SAID WHAT?!

d. **Speaking Only When Necessary:** By speaking only when necessary, one can cultivate a sense of mindfulness and restraint. This can be done by avoiding unnecessary chatter or idle talk and speaking only when there is a clear purpose or benefit to the conversation.

In summary, Right Speech is about speaking truthfully, kindly, and constructively. It involves avoiding lying, gossiping, harsh language, and idle chatter, and speaking only when necessary and in a way that is beneficial to others. By practicing Right Speech, one can cultivate a sense of integrity, harmony, and goodwill towards others, leading to greater happiness and well-being.

4. **Right Action** is the fourth step of the Noble Eightfold Path. It refers to behaving in ways that are morally and ethically sound and that promote the well-being of oneself and others. It is about cultivating positive behaviors and avoiding harmful ones. This practice involves behaving in a way that is ethical, compassionate, and in line with our values and beliefs. It is about making choices that benefit others, avoiding harmful behaviors, and living in a way that aligns with our deepest values. In order to practice Right Action, we must first cultivate awareness of our own actions and their consequences. We must recognize when our actions are motivated by harmful intentions or have the potential to cause harm to others. We must also be mindful of our behavior, making sure that it is in line with the principles of non-harm, non-violence, and respect for all living beings. In real life, there are many examples of how

the practice of Right Action can be applied. For instance, if we are tempted to steal or cheat in order to gain an advantage, we may cause harm to others and damage our own integrity. However, if we cultivate Right Action, we can recognize the harm that such actions would cause and instead behave in ways that are honest, fair, and respectful of others. Another example of how Right Action can be applied is in our relationships with others. If we are prone to anger or violence, we may cause harm to others and damage our own relationships. However, if we cultivate Right Action, we can recognize the harm that such behaviors would cause,and instead behave in ways that are peaceful, respectful, and compassionate.

The practice of Right Action is about cultivating positive behaviors and avoiding harmful ones in order to promote the well-being of oneself and others. By cultivating this practice, we can reduce our own suffering and others suffering and move towards a state of enlightenment and liberation. In Buddhism, Right Action is one of the Noble Eightfold Path's steps, which leads to liberation from suffering and the attainment of enlightenment. Right Action is about acting in a way that is ethical, responsible, and compassionate towards all beings. The Buddha defined Right Action as abstaining from actions that harm others, such as killing, stealing, and sexual misconduct. Instead, one should act in ways that promote the well-being of others and the world around them. Here are some examples of how Right Action can be practiced in daily life:

a. **Practicing Non-violence:** By practicing non-violence, one can cultivate a sense of compassion and empathy towards all beings. This can be done by avoiding actions that harm others, such as physical violence or verbal abuse, and instead choosing to act with kindness and understanding.

b. **Respecting The Property of Others:** By respecting the property of others, one can cultivate a sense of responsibility and fairness. This can be done by avoiding stealing or taking what does not belong to oneself and instead choosing to act with honesty and integrity.

c. **Acting with Sexual Restraint:** By acting with sexual restraint, one can cultivate a sense of respect and mindfulness. This can be done by avoiding sexual misconduct, such as engaging in sexual relationships that harm others or oneself, and instead choosing to act with compassion and understanding.

d. **Practicing Generosity:** By practicing generosity, one can cultivate a sense of selflessness and altruism. We can do this by giving, volunteering, or being kind.

In summary, Right Action is about acting in a way that is ethical, responsible, and compassionate towards all beings. It involves abstaining from actions that harm others and choosing to act in ways that promote the well-being of others and the world around them. By practicing Right Action, one can cultivate a sense of responsibility, compassion, and ethical awareness, leading to greater happiness and well-being.

5. **Right Livelihood** is the fifth step of the Noble Eightfold Path. It refers to earning a livelihood in ways that are ethical, responsible, and do not cause

harm to oneself or others. It is about recognizing the impact of our work and livelihood on the world around us and striving to make positive contributions to society. This practice involves making a living in a way that is ethical, does not harm others, and is in line with our values and beliefs. It is about finding work that is meaningful and fulfilling and that contributes to the well-being of ourselves and others. In order to practice Right Livelihood, we must first cultivate awareness of our own work and its impact on the world around us. We must recognize when our work is motivated by greed or harmful intentions and strive to find ways to earn a living that are in line with the principles of non-harm and non-violence. In real life, there are many examples of how the practice of Right Livelihood can be applied. For instance, if we work in a business that profits from unethical or harmful practices, such as the exploitation of workers or environmental degradation, we may be contributing to the suffering of others and the destruction of the planet. However, if we cultivate Right Livelihood, we can recognize the harm that such practices would cause and instead seek out work that is responsible, sustainable, and aligned with our values. Another example of how Right Livelihood can be applied is in our personal consumption habits. If we consume products that are produced using unethical or harmful practices, we may be contributing to the suffering of others and the destruction of the planet. However, if we cultivate Right Livelihood, we can recognize the harm that such practices would cause and instead seek out products that are produced in ways that are responsible, sustainable, and aligned with our values.

The practice of Right Livelihood is about earning a livelihood in ways that are ethical, responsible, and do not cause harm to oneself or others. By cultivating this practice, we can reduce our own suffering and the suffering of others, and move towards a state of enlightenment and liberation.

In Buddhism, Right Livelihood is about choosing a profession or occupation that is ethical, responsible, and beneficial to others. The Buddha defined Right Livelihood as abstaining from occupations that harm others or the environment, such as selling weapons, dealing in drugs or alcohol, or engaging in any business that causes harm to living beings. Instead, one should choose a livelihood that promotes the well-being of others and contributes to the greater good. Here are some examples of how Right Livelihood can be practiced in daily life:

a. **Engaging in a Profession That Helps Others:** By engaging in a profession that helps others, one can cultivate a sense of altruism and compassion. This can be done by pursuing a career in healthcare, social work, education, or any other profession that benefits society and promotes the well-being of others.

b. **Choose an Eco-friendly Profession:** By choosing a profession that is environmentally responsible, one can cultivate a sense of responsibility and awareness towards the environment. This can be done by pursuing a career in renewable energy, conservation, sustainable agriculture, or any other profession that contributes to the protection and preservation of the natural world.

c. **Avoiding Occupations That Harm Others:** By avoiding occupations that harm others, one can cultivate a sense of ethical awareness and responsibility. This can be done by refraining from engaging in businesses that promote violence, exploitation, or any other form of harm to living beings.

d. **Pursuing a Career That Aligns with One's Values:** By pursuing a career that aligns with one's values, one can cultivate a sense of purpose and fulfillment. This can be done by choosing a profession that is aligned with one's personal values, beliefs, and aspirations.

In summary, Right Livelihood is about choosing a profession or occupation that is ethical, responsible, and beneficial to others. It involves abstaining from occupations that harm others or the environment and choosing a livelihood that promotes the well-being of others and contributes to the greater good. By practicing Right Livelihood, one can cultivate a sense of responsibility, compassion, and ethical awareness, leading to greater happiness and well-being.

The third category of the Noble Eightfold Path is *Mental Development*, which includes the final three practices:

6. **Right Effort** is the sixth step of the Noble Eightfold Path. This practice involves making a consistent effort to cultivate positive qualities such as compassion, generosity, and wisdom and to overcome negative qualities such as greed, hatred, and delusion. It is about working diligently to transform ourselves and our habits and to develop the qualities that will lead

to lasting happiness and well-being. Right Effort is the path to achieving liberation from suffering and attaining enlightenment. It is about making an effort to cultivate positive qualities and eliminate negative ones. It involves putting forth the right amount of effort in the right direction, with the right attitude.

The Buddha described Right Effort as having four aspects:

a. **Preventing Unwholesome States of Mind From Arising:** One way to prevent unwholesome states of mind, such as anger or jealousy, from arising is to be mindful of one's thoughts and emotions. This can be done through meditation or simply by being aware of one's thoughts throughout the day. When a negative thought arises, one can make an effort to let it go and focus on something positive instead.

b. **Abandoning Unwholesome States of Mind That Have Already Arisen:** If an unwholesome state of mind has already arisen, such as anger towards someone, one can make an effort to let go of it and not dwell on it. This can be done through meditation or by focusing on positive qualities of the person instead of their negative actions.

c. **Cultivating Wholesome States of Mind That Have Not Yet Arisen:** One can cultivate wholesome states of mind, such as compassion or generosity, through intentional actions. For example, one can make an effort to donate to charity or volunteer their time to help others.

d. **Maintaining and Developing Wholesome States of Mind That Have Already Arisen:**

Once wholesome states of mind have arisen, such as a sense of peace or contentment, one can make an effort to maintain and develop them. This can be done through continued meditation or by engaging in activities that bring about positive emotions.

In summary, Right Effort is about making a conscious effort to cultivate positive qualities and eliminate negative ones. It involves being mindful of one's thoughts and emotions, letting go of unwholesome states of mind, and intentionally cultivating wholesome ones. By practicing Right Effort, one can gradually develop a more positive and peaceful state of mind, which is a key component of the Buddhist path towards liberation from suffering.

7. **Right Mindfulness** is the seventh step of the Noble Eightfold Path. This practice involves cultivating a state of awareness and acceptance in the present moment and developing a deeper understanding of our thoughts, emotions, and experiences. It is about being fully present in each moment and developing the ability to observe our own mind and its workings with clarity and compassion. Right Mindfulness leads to liberation from suffering and the attainment of enlightenment. Right Mindfulness is the ability to be present in the present moment and to be fully aware of one's thoughts, feelings, and surroundings without judgment.

The Buddha defined Right Mindfulness as having four foundations:

a. **Mindfulness of The Body:** One can practice mindfulness of the body by being aware of the sensations that arise during daily activities. For example, when walking, one can focus on the feeling of the feet touching the ground or the sensation of the wind on the skin.

b. **Mindfulness of Feelings:** One can practice mindfulness of feelings by being aware of the various emotions that arise in response to events and situations. For example, if one feels angry, instead of reacting impulsively, one can take a moment to observe and acknowledge the anger before deciding how to respond.

c. **Mindfulness of The Mind:** One can practice mindfulness of the mind by being aware of one's thoughts and mental states. For example, when feeling anxious or worried, one can observe the thoughts and feelings that arise and acknowledge them without judgment.

d. **Mindfulness of Mental Objects:** One can practice mindfulness of mental objects by being aware of the various perceptions and intentions that arise during daily activities. For example, when talking to someone, one can be mindful of their own intentions and the other person's perceptions.

In summary, Right Mindfulness is about being fully present and aware of one's thoughts, feelings, and surroundings without judgment. It involves being mindful of the body, feelings, mind, and mental objects. By practicing Right Mindfulness, one can develop a deeper understanding of oneself and the world, leading to greater peace and happiness.

8. **Right Concentration** is the last step of the Noble Eightfold Path. This practice involves cultivating the ability to focus our mind and develop a deep and sustained level of concentration, which can lead to states of insight and enlightenment. It is about training our minds to be calm and focused and to develop the clarity and wisdom that will allow us to see the world as it truly is. In Buddhism, which leads to the liberation from suffering and the attainment of enlightenment. Right Concentration is the ability to focus one's mind on a single object or task without distraction. The Buddha defined Right Concentration as the practice of Jhana, which involves a deep state of meditation that leads to the purification of the mind and the elimination of negative mental states.

Here are some examples of how Right Concentration can be practiced in daily life:

a. **Meditation:**
    Meditation is a powerful tool for developing Right Concentration. One can start by setting aside a few minutes each day to sit in a quiet place and focus on the breath. By practicing regularly, one can develop the ability to concentrate the mind and enter deeper states of meditation.

b. **Engaging in a Single Task:**
    Engaging in a single task, such as cooking, cleaning, or gardening, can be a form of Right Concentration. By focusing one's attention on the task at hand and being fully present in the

THE BUDDHA SAID WHAT?!

moment, one can cultivate a sense of calm and inner peace.

c. **Practicing Mindfulness:**
    Practicing mindfulness is another way to develop Right Concentration. By being fully present and aware of one's thoughts, feelings, and surroundings without judgment, one can cultivate a deep sense of concentration and focus.

d. **Deepening One's Spiritual Practice:**
    Deepening one's spiritual practice, such as through reading spiritual texts or attending religious services, can also be a form of Right Concentration. By focusing one's attention on the teachings and practices of one's chosen tradition, one can cultivate a deep sense of inner peace and spiritual insight.

In summary, Right Concentration is about the ability to focus one's mind on a single object or task without distraction. It involves the practice of Jhana, deep states of meditation that lead to the purification of the mind and the elimination of negative mental states. By practicing Right Concentration, one can cultivate a deep sense of calm and inner peace, leading to greater happiness and well-being.

Walk the Path Daily

Incorporating the Noble Eightfold Path into your daily life can be a transformative experience, helping you to cultivate a deeper sense of mindfulness, ethical responsibility, and compassion. Each of the eight components offers a unique opportunity to tap into your innermost being and connect with the world around you in a more meaningful way. Whether you start by focusing on one or two components that resonate with you or dive headfirst into the entire path, the journey towards living a more mindful and compassionate life can be both challenging and rewarding. With each step forward, you'll find yourself growing more aware of your thoughts, actions, and intentions and building stronger, more meaningful relationships with those around you. Above all, it's important to remember that the Noble Eightfold Path is not a set of rigid rules to be followed blindly, but rather a flexible set of guidelines designed to help you discover your own unique path towards enlightenment. As you navigate the challenges and joys of life, let the Noble Eightfold Path be your guide, helping you to cultivate the wisdom, insight, and compassion you need to truly thrive. It's important to note that practicing mindfulness is a fundamental aspect of the Noble Eightfold Path. In the upcoming chapter, we'll delve deeper into the practice of mindfulness and explore ways to apply it in our daily lives. By incorporating mindfulness into our routine, we can cultivate a greater awareness of our thoughts and emotions, develop a deeper sense of inner peace, and improve our overall well-being. So stay tuned as we embark on this journey towards greater mindfulness and self-awareness.

6

MINDFULNESS

I N THE previous chapter, we learned that mindfulness is fundamental to the Noble Eightfold Path because it serves as a cornerstone for developing awareness, insight, and a deep understanding of oneself and the world. Through the practice of mindfulness, we cultivate a heightened sense of present-moment awareness, observing our thoughts, emotions, sensations, and surroundings without judgment or attachment. This practice allows us to develop a clearer understanding of the impermanent and interconnected nature of reality and helps us become more skilled in our thoughts, speech, and actions. Mindfulness supports the other aspects of the Noble Eightfold Path, such as Right View, Right Intention, Right Speech, Right Action, and Right Concentration, by promoting an attentive and non-reactive state of mind. By cultivating mindfulness, we can gain a deeper insight into the nature of suffering, the causes of suffering, and the path leading to the cessation of suffering. In this chapter, we will delve deeper into mindfulness, exploring its practices and benefits to help us achieve our goals more effectively.

The Power of Now

Mindfulness involves being fully present and engaged in the current moment without judgment or distraction. In meditation, mindfulness allows us to focus our attention on our breath, thoughts, or other sensations while letting go of distractions and interruptions. By practicing mindfulness in meditation, we develop our ability to focus and concentrate, and we become more aware of our thoughts and emotions. This increased awareness can help us understand ourselves better and develop more compassion and empathy for others. Mindfulness meditation has been proven through research to offer numerous benefits for both physical and mental health, including reduced stress, anxiety, and depression, improved sleep quality, cognitive function, and overall well-being. The importance of mindfulness in meditation lies in its ability to help us enhance our focus and be fully present in the moment. This heightened awareness can lead to better self-understanding, improved mental and physical health, and the cultivation of greater compassion and empathy for others. Studies have found that mindfulness can help improve both mental and physical health.

Regular practice of mindfulness has been shown to have positive effects on mental well-being, including a reduction in symptoms of anxiety, depression, and stress. A study conducted by Hofmann and his team in 2010 examined forty-seven mindfulness-based intervention studies and their effects on mental well-being. The researchers found that practicing mindfulness led to notable reductions in symptoms of anxiety and depression among participants. The study highlighted the potential of mindfulness as an effective approach for improving psychological health. The findings provided empirical support for the beneficial impact of mindfulness-based interventions on mental well-being and further reinforced the importance of incorporating mindfulness practices into therapeutic and self-care routines. In addition to its impact on mental well-being, mindfulness has been found to offer various benefits for cognitive function, such as memory, attention, and decision-making. A study conducted by Jha and his team in 2010 explored the effects of mindfulness meditation practice on cognitive abilities. The findings revealed that participants who engaged in mindfulness meditation demonstrated improvements in cognitive flexibility and working memory capacity. This suggests that regular mindfulness practice can positively influence cognitive functioning and enhance abilities related to attention, memory, and decision-making.

Mindfulness not only benefits mental and cognitive well-being but also has a positive impact on physical health. A study by Cherkin and his team in 2016 showed that mindfulness-based stress reduction can help reduce chronic pain. Participants who practiced mindfulness reported a decrease in their pain levels. This suggests that mindfulness is beneficial for those seeking relief from persistent pain. Additionally, research has found that mindfulness can improve blood pressure control, potentially lowering high blood pressure. Moreover, mindfulness has a positive impact on sleep quality, helping individuals achieve better and more rejuvenating sleep. These findings demonstrate the potential of mindfulness as a holistic approach to improving physical well-being and managing various health conditions. Furthermore, research has indicated that mindfulness practice can have positive effects on the immune system and reduce inflammation in the body. A study conducted by Davidson and his team in 2003 provided evidence supporting these benefits. The study found that individuals who engaged in mindfulness meditation showed increased activity in brain regions associated with positive emotions and immune system functioning. Additionally, these individuals displayed reduced levels of pro-inflammatory markers in their blood. These findings suggest that mindfulness practice may contribute to improved immune system functioning and the reduction of inflammation. By incorporating mindfulness into our lives, we can potentially enhance our overall health and well-being.

Overall, there is a growing body of research that suggests that mindfulness can have numerous benefits for both mental and physical health. Furthermore, many large organizations have recognized the benefits of mindfulness and have incorporated mindfulness training into their staff training programs. Here are a few examples:

- **Google:** Google offers a mindfulness program called "Search Inside Yourself" which teaches mindfulness, emotional intelligence, and leadership skills to employees. The program has been found to improve employee well-being, reduce stress, and increase focus and productivity.
- **Apple:** Apple offers mindfulness training to its employees through a program called "Mindful Minutes." The program includes guided meditations and other mindfulness practices to help employees reduce stress and improve focus.
- **General Mills:** General Mills offers a mindfulness program called "Mindful Leadership" which helps employees develop mindfulness skills to improve their leadership abilities. The program has been found to increase productivity, reduce absenteeism, and improve employee engagement.
- **Aetna:** Aetna offers a mindfulness program called "Mindfulness at Work" which teaches employees

how to incorporate mindfulness into their daily work routines. The program has been found to reduce stress and improve employee well-being.

Mindfulness training can bring a range of benefits to employees in different businesses, contributing to their well-being, performance, and overall job satisfaction. Some of these benefits include:

- **Stress Reduction:** Mindfulness training helps employees develop techniques to manage stress more effectively. It promotes self-awareness, resilience, and the ability to stay calm and focused in challenging situations.
- **Improved Focus and Productivity:** Mindfulness enhances attention and concentration, allowing employees to stay more engaged and focused on their tasks. This increased focus can lead to improved productivity and efficiency in the workplace.
- **Enhanced Emotional Intelligence:** Mindfulness cultivates emotional intelligence by developing self-awareness and empathy. Employees become better equipped to understand their own emotions and the emotions of others, leading to improved interpersonal relationships and communication.
- **Better Decision Making:** Mindfulness practices help employees develop clearer and more objective thinking, enabling them to make better decisions based on present-moment awareness and a broader perspective.
- **Increased Creativity and Innovation:** Mindfulness fosters a mindset of curiosity, open-mindedness, and non-judgment, which are conducive to creativity and

innovation. Employees are more likely to generate new ideas and think outside the box.

- **Improved Work-Life Balance:** Mindfulness helps employees create a healthier work-life balance by promoting present-moment awareness and reducing the tendency to ruminate on work-related issues during personal time. This leads to increased satisfaction and well-being both inside and outside of work.

- **Enhanced Team Collaboration:** Mindfulness training encourages active listening, empathy, and open communication, fostering a positive team environment and promoting collaboration among employees.

- **Increased Resilience:** Mindfulness cultivates mental and emotional resilience, enabling employees to bounce back more quickly from setbacks or challenges. It helps them manage change, adapt to new situations, and maintain a positive attitude.

Overall, mindfulness training can be a valuable tool for large organizations looking to improve employee well-being, productivity, and engagement. By incorporating mindfulness into their training programs, these organizations can create a more positive and supportive work environment and foster greater creativity and innovation among their staff. The practice of mindfulness is often associated with meditation, but it can also be applied to everyday activities like eating, walking, or washing dishes. By bringing full attention and intention to these activities, we can cultivate mindfulness and deepen our spiritual practice. In addition, mindfulness meditation is a powerful tool for overcoming the ego and achieving inner peace. It is a specific form of meditation that involves paying attention to the present moment with non-judgmental

THE BUDDHA SAID WHAT?!

awareness. It is based on the Buddhist practice of Sati, which means "mindfulness" or "awareness". During mindfulness meditation, we focus our attention on a particular object, such as the breath, a sound, or a physical sensation. Whenever the mind wanders, the practitioner gently brings our attention back to the chosen object without judgment or criticism.

Mindfulness Meditation

To practice mindfulness meditation, find a quiet and comfortable place where you can sit or lie down without being disturbed. Set a timer for the desired length of your practice, and begin by focusing on your chosen object. Whenever your mind wanders, gently bring your attention back to the object without judgment or criticism. If you wish to practice mindfulness meditation centered around synchronizing the movement of your stomach with your breath, you may follow these instructions:

- **Step 1:** Find a quiet and comfortable space. Choose a peaceful environment where you can sit without interruptions. You can sit on a cushion, chair, or any surface that allows you to maintain an upright and relaxed posture.
- **Step 2:** Assume a comfortable position. Sit with your back straight but not rigid, allowing your body to be at ease. Rest your hands on your lap or thighs, whichever feels comfortable for you. Close your eyes gently or keep a soft gaze.
- **Step 3:** Center yourself with a few deep breaths. Take a few deep breaths to ground yourself in the present moment. Allow any tension or distractions to melt away as you exhale slowly.

- **Step 4:** Direct your attention to the stomach. Shift your focus to the natural movement of your stomach as you breathe in and out. Notice the sensation of the stomach rising and falling with each breath.
- **Step 5:** Anchor your attention to the stomach. Use the movement of the stomach as your anchor for attention. As you inhale, feel the expansion and gentle rise of the stomach. As you exhale, feel the relaxation and gentle descent of the stomach.
- **Step 6:** Stay present with the movement. Maintain your focus on the stomach's movement, staying present with each breath. If your mind starts to wander, gently bring your attention back to the sensation of your stomach rising and falling.
- **Step 7:** Cultivate non-judgmental awareness. Allow the experience to unfold without judgment or criticism. If thoughts, emotions, or sensations arise, acknowledge them without getting caught up in them and gently return your attention to the movement of the stomach.
- **Step 8:** Continue for a specific duration. Set a timer or decide on a designated time for your meditation practice. Start with shorter sessions, such as 5–10 minutes, and gradually extend the duration as you become more comfortable.
- **Step 9:** Conclude the practice. When you're ready to end the meditation, take a few moments to transition out of the practice. Gently open your eyes, stretch your body, and carry the sense of mindfulness and presence into the rest of your day.

Remember, mindfulness meditation is a skill that develops over time with regular practice. Be patient and kind to yourself as you cultivate your ability to stay focused on the movement of the stomach and the breath. Overall, practicing mindfulness meditation involves focusing your attention on the present moment with non-judgmental awareness. By cultivating this skill, you can develop greater insight, self-awareness, and inner peace and reduce stress and anxiety in your daily life. Over time, with regular practice, mindfulness meditation can become a valuable tool for improving mental and emotional well-being and cultivating greater awareness and presence in your daily life.

There are two primary approaches to practicing mindfulness: through mindful meditation and by engaging in mindful everyday activities.

The first approach is **mindful meditation**, which is a powerful technique that has been used for centuries to cultivate inner peace and clarity of mind. This form of meditation involves setting aside a specific time and space to engage in deep introspection and self-awareness. Usually, practitioners assume a comfortable seated or lying-down position with their eyes closed, creating a peaceful and distraction-free environment for reflection. During mindful meditation, we focus on observing and accepting our thoughts, emotions, and sensations as they arise, without any judgment or reaction. The practice involves redirecting our attention back to the present moment whenever the mind wanders, helping us to develop greater mindfulness and self-awareness. The benefits of mindful meditation are many. For example, regular practice can help reduce stress, anxiety, and depression, increase focus and productivity, improve emotional regulation, and enhance overall well-being. Mindful meditation can also help develop greater compassion and empathy, leading to more positive and fulfilling relationships with others. Mindful meditation is a valuable tool for anyone seeking to cultivate greater inner peace, clarity of mind, and overall well-being. By setting aside time each day to engage in deep introspection and self-awareness, we can develop greater mindfulness and self-awareness, leading to a more fulfilling and satisfying life.

Mindful everyday activities is another approach to mindfulness that can be easily integrated into daily life. It can also be practiced during everyday activities such as walking, eating, or washing dishes. The focus is on bringing awareness to the present moment experience of the activity, observing sensations, thoughts, and emotions as they arise, and bringing attention back to the activity whenever the mind wanders. This practice can help cultivate greater presence, appreciation, and enjoyment of everyday experiences. For instance, when walking mindfully, the focus is on the sensation of the feet touching the ground, the feeling of the wind against the skin, and the sights and sounds in the environment. While eating, we can focus on the texture and flavor of the food, the sensation of chewing and swallowing, and the feeling of fullness in the stomach. Mindful everyday activities can help cultivate greater presence, appreciation, and enjoyment of daily experiences. It can also help us be more fully engaged in the activities we are performing, reducing distractions and improving overall productivity. In conclusion, mindful everyday activities are an excellent way to integrate mindfulness into daily life. By bringing focused awareness to everyday activities, we can cultivate greater presence, appreciation, and enjoyment of daily experiences, leading to a more fulfilling and satisfying life.

Both of these methods can be effective ways to cultivate mindfulness and bring greater awareness to your present moment experience. They can be adapted to suit your individual needs and preferences and can be practiced anywhere, at any time. With regular practice, you may find that mindfulness becomes a natural part of your daily life, helping you to manage stress, improve focus and productivity, and cultivate greater well-being and happiness. Mindfulness is important to everyday life because it allows us to be fully present in each moment, to reduce stress and anxiety, to improve our relationships, to cultivate a sense of purpose and meaning, and to enhance our overall well-being. In Buddhism, mindfulness is considered a crucial component of the path to enlightenment. The Buddha taught that mindfulness is essential for understanding the nature of reality and cultivating wisdom and compassion. At its heart, mindfulness is about paying attention to the present moment with curiosity and without judgment. Rather than getting caught up in thoughts about the past or worries about the future, mindfulness encourages us to be fully present in the here and now. Mindfulness has become increasingly popular in the modern world as a way to reduce stress and anxiety and improve mental well-being. At its core, mindfulness is about being present in the moment and fully aware of one's thoughts, feelings, and surroundings.

One of the key teachings of Buddhism is the impermanence of all things. Everything in life is constantly changing, and nothing is permanent. Mindfulness helps us recognize and accept this truth rather than resisting or denying it. By being fully present in each moment, we can learn to appreciate the beauty and richness of life, even in the midst of difficulties. Another important aspect of mindfulness is self-awareness. By paying attention to our thoughts and emotions without judgment, we can begin to understand ourselves more deeply. We can observe our habitual patterns of thought and behavior and begin to make changes that lead to greater happiness and fulfillment. Mindfulness is seen as a key tool for achieving inner peace and enlightenment, as it helps practitioners cultivate awareness and detachment from their thoughts and emotions.

By observing the workings of the mind without getting caught up in them, Buddhists believe that they can overcome the illusion of ego and achieve a state of pure awareness and compassion. By embracing presence and impermanence, we transcend suffering from attachment and aversion. We can learn to live in the world with greater wisdom, compassion, and understanding and to cultivate a deep sense of connection to ourselves and others. In the upcoming chapter, we will discover the methods for practicing meditation and explore its significance.

7

MEDITATION

H AVE YOU ever considered why there has been a recent increase in people seeking to learn meditation? Have you personally experienced the transformative effects that meditation can bring to your life? Are you aware that mindfulness training is a crucial component of meditation? Have you ever wondered why large corporations invest in mindfulness training? What about children with special needs? Can mindfulness practices help them achieve the inner calm and concentration they require to manage their day-to-day routines? Are you aware of the wide range of benefits that meditation can bring?

Considering these points, what do you believe are the main objectives of meditation?

Integrating Meditation into Daily Life

There are several reasons why practicing meditation can be beneficial. Meditation offers an opportunity to cultivate inner peace, self-discovery, and a deeper connection with yourself and the world around you. It is a valuable tool for personal growth, well-being, and living a more fulfilling life. The reason for the growing interest in meditation among people these days could be attributed to the increasing recognition of the advantages that meditation provides for mental and physical health. In meditation, mindfulness is cultivated through the practice of focused attention or open awareness. Through mindfulness training, we can learn to develop a greater awareness of our mental and emotional states, as well as our physical sensations and surroundings. This increased awareness can help cultivate a sense of inner peace, reduce stress and anxiety, and improve overall well-being. In the previous chapter, we discovered that major organizations today increasingly appreciate the remarkable benefits that mindfulness training, an essential component of meditation, can bring to their businesses, such as reducing stress levels, improving productivity, and enhancing work relationships. This can lead to significant benefits that cannot be measured solely in terms of financial gain. When it comes to personal reasons, such as with special needs children, it is vital that we provide them with the necessary tools to achieve a sense of inner peace. The advantages of mindfulness training for children with special needs are substantial, including improved focus and attention as well as better emotional regulation and behavior. Do you think it is acceptable to disregard a powerful tool that can potentially bring immense positive changes to the lives of children? Mindfulness training has been extensively researched and has been shown to be highly effective. The valuable practice of mindfulness training should be accessible to every child, irrespective of their needs, so that they can benefit from it.

According to Buddhist teachings, the primary purpose of meditation is to cultivate inner peace and happiness. True joy can be found within the mind, and meditation is a way to access the deep sense of peace and happiness that resides within each person. By practicing meditation, Buddhists seek to calm their minds, cultivate positive states of being, and ultimately attain enlightenment. For example, a layperson might incorporate meditation into their daily routine as a means of reducing stress, increasing focus, and improving their overall mental and emotional health. Similarly, a Buddhist monk might spend hours each day in meditation, focusing their attention on their breath and allowing their thoughts and emotions to pass without attachment or judgment. Through this practice, they may gradually develop greater mindfulness, emotional regulation, and equanimity, ultimately leading them to attain enlightenment.

Two Common Meditation Practices

In the context of Buddhism, there exist two distinct forms of meditation: **Samatha (Calming)**, which prioritizes a calm and peaceful state of mind, and **Vipassana (Insight)**, which emphasizes insight and mindfulness. In this chapter, you will gain an understanding of how to practice vipassana meditation, which can lead to a heightened awareness of the interdependence and transience of all phenomena, including the body and mind. Furthermore, vipassana meditation can facilitate the development of profound insight and wisdom into the essential nature of existence and ultimately empower you to attain freedom from suffering.

Do you think that material possessions like luxury cars or money can provide the same level of happiness as inner peace? Is it possible for wealthy individuals to achieve perpetual happiness and avoid all forms of suffering in their lives? If so, why do some people who live a seemingly wonderful life struggle to live it to the fullest due to poor health or a shortened lifespan? If money is the solution to all problems, then why do countless people dedicate their lives to earning a lot of money, only to pass away before they can fully reap the rewards of their hard work or experience the world? Have you ever heard the story of Ranjan Das? He was a well-known Indian business executive and the CEO of SAP India. Das was known for his exceptional work ethic and dedication to his job. He earned high respect from colleagues and was credited with revitalizing SAP India's business. He has achieved great success in his career and is leading a fulfilling life. He prioritizes his health by abstaining from drinking and smoking and maintaining a healthy lifestyle. Das often worked long hours per day, slept only a few hours at night, and rarely took vacations. Unfortunately, this demanding lifestyle took a toll on his health. In October 2009, after a workout, he collapsed and was rushed to the hospital, where he passed away at the young age of forty-two due to cardiac arrest.

Even though many people believe that money and success can bring happiness, they are unable to prevent us from experiencing bad health or death. The story of Das serves as an example of this. Despite his accomplishments in all areas of life, he still suffered from poor health and eventually passed away. Working hard and getting less sleep can contribute to stress. When we work hard, our bodies and minds are under constant pressure, which can lead to exhaustion and burnout. If we do not get enough sleep, it can make it harder for our bodies to recover and our minds to function properly. This can lead to increased stress levels as we struggle to keep up with our work and other responsibilities. Das may have been unaware of the negative effects that result from overworking himself. His lack of rest, relaxation, and stress-reducing mindfulness practices could have had an impact on his overall well-being. Over the years, research has shown that meditation can have numerous benefits for both physical health and mental well-being. Here are some of the ways in which meditation can help:

- **Reduced Stress and Anxiety:** Studies have found that meditation can help reduce stress and anxiety, which can have a positive impact on overall health. By practicing meditation, we may be able to reduce cortisol levels, a hormone that is associated with stress, and improve our ability to cope with challenging situations.

- **Improved Sleep:** Meditation has also been found to improve sleep quality, which is important for physical health and mental well-being. By calming the mind and body, meditation can help us fall asleep faster and stay asleep longer.

- **Lowered Blood Pressure:** Another benefit of meditation is that it can lower blood pressure, which is important for heart health. Research has found that regular meditation can lead to lower blood pressure in people with hypertension.

- **Increased Immunity:** Meditation may also have a positive impact on the immune system, helping to protect the body against illness and disease. Studies have found that regular meditation can increase activity in the part of the brain that is responsible for producing antibodies.

* **Improved Mental Health:** In addition to physical health benefits, meditation has also been shown to have positive effects on mental health. By reducing stress and anxiety, meditation can improve overall mood and well-being. Additionally, research has found that meditation can be an effective tool for managing symptoms of depression and anxiety.

According to the research, we may be able to improve our overall well-being and quality of life by incorporating regular meditation into our daily routines. Das shows us that material possessions and achievements alone cannot guarantee a fulfilling life. While money and luxury possessions may provide temporary happiness, they cannot match the lasting contentment that comes from inner peace. While having wealth may provide a comfortable lifestyle, it does not guarantee protection from all forms of suffering or ensure perpetual happiness. Like everyone else, those who are wealthy may face personal challenges, health issues, or setbacks that can impact their overall well-being. Happiness cannot be bought with money or possessions; it originates from within. Though money and luxury items can offer fleeting pleasure, lasting happiness stems from inner peace. Hence, a balanced life that encompasses both material possessions and spiritual growth is crucial. The story of the Buddha also serves as a powerful illustration of this concept. Despite leading a privileged life, he was still not content and longed to discover the path to true happiness. It was only when he sat under the Bodhi tree and engaged in deep meditation that he was able to access the inner peace and happiness that had always resided within him. But you don't have to be a spiritual leader to benefit from meditation. Countless people have found profound joy and

THE BUDDHA SAID WHAT?!

contentment through regular meditation practice. By taking time to quiet the mind and focus on the present moment, we can access the deep well of peace and happiness that resides within us all.

Buddhists meditate to find inner peace and happiness. Meditation allows them to tap into a deep well of tranquility and joy within themselves, considering inner peace the ultimate form of joy. As previously mentioned, Samatha (calming) and Vipassana (insight) are two types of meditation practiced in Buddhism. Let's delve into more detail about each of them.

Samatha Meditation

Samatha meditation involves developing a calm, clear, and concentrated mind. The word "Samatha" in Pali means "tranquility" or "calmness". The main objective of this meditation practice is to calm and focus the mind, leading to a state of deep relaxation and inner peace. In Samatha meditation, the practitioner focuses their attention on a single object, such as the breath, a sound, or an image. By focusing on this object, the mind becomes still and distractions are reduced, leading to a state of deep relaxation. Through consistent practice, the mind becomes more focused and concentrated, allowing the practitioner to experience a greater sense of peace and tranquility. In addition to its calming benefits, Samatha meditation can also improve mental and physical health. Studies have shown that regular practice can lead to a reduction in stress, anxiety, and depression, as well as improvements in focus, attention, and overall well-being. Samatha meditation is commonly used as a preparation for vipassana meditation, which is a form of insight meditation that emphasizes developing wisdom and insight into the fundamental nature of reality.

Vipassana Meditation

Vipassana meditation, also known as insight meditation, is a key meditation practice in Buddhism. The word "vipassana" in Pali means "seeing things as they really are". Vipassana meditation involves the cultivation of mindfulness and awareness of the present moment in order to gain insight into the true nature of reality. The practice of vipassana meditation aims to deepen the understanding of the Three Universal Truths in Buddhism: impermanence, suffering, and non-self. By observing the changing nature of phenomena within and outside of oneself, a practitioner can begin to develop a more profound insight into the nature of existence and the causes of suffering. The practice of vipassana involves a variety of techniques, including body scanning, breath meditation, and observing mental states and emotions. Through these techniques, meditators can begin to observe the constant flux and impermanence of all things, including their own thoughts and emotions. The ultimate goal of vipassana meditation is to attain a state of liberation or enlightenment, in which one gains a deep understanding of the true nature of existence and transcends the cycle of suffering. This state is achieved through the cultivation of wisdom, compassion, and mindfulness in everyday life. Vipassana meditation is often practiced in conjunction with Samatha meditation to achieve a balanced and integrated approach to meditation practice. When practiced together, these two types of meditation can help cultivate a balanced and peaceful mind, which is essential for spiritual growth and well-being.

Our primary emphasis in this section will be on the practice of vipassana meditation. Firstly, it is essential to understand that humans consist of both a physical body and a mind. The physical form, which is temporary and impermanent, is subject to aging, illness, and death. In contrast, the mind is viewed as the source of feelings, memories, thoughts, and consciousness. The practice of Vipassana meditation typically involves key components, including:

1. **Mindfulness of The Breath:** Mindfulness of the breath involves paying attention to the breath's movement through the nostrils and the rising and falling of the stomach with each inhale and exhale. This practice requires focusing on the sensation of the breath entering and leaving the body or the movement of the stomach as you breathe. During the practice of vipassana meditation, it is recommended to focus on observing the rise and fall of the stomach instead of the flow of breath from the nose, as it is easier to detect and maintain focus on. As a foundational practice in developing concentration and calmness of the mind, mindfulness of the stomach's movement is commonly utilized. Focusing on sustained and non-judgmental awareness of the movement of the stomach is a form of mindfulness meditation that can help reduce distraction and improve concentration.

    Exercise:

    1. Find a comfortable sitting position.
    2. Straighten your back.
    3. Slowly close your eyes.
    4. Observe the rise and fall of your stomach with each inhalation and exhalation.

5. Be aware that your mind is recognizing the movement of your body.
6. Recognize that the body and mind work independently.
7. Repeat steps 4-6 for 10–15 minutes each day.

The length of time recommended for mindfulness meditation practice varies depending on your preferences and schedule. It is generally recommended to start with shorter sessions, such as 5–10 minutes a day, and gradually increase the duration as you become more comfortable with the practice. Some people practice mindfulness meditation for 20–30 minutes a day, while others may meditate for longer periods of time. The most important thing is to establish a consistent daily practice, even if it is just for a few minutes. As you continue to practice mindfulness meditation through the movement of the stomach, you may begin to notice a number of benefits. Here are some examples:

- **Increased Focus and Concentration:** By training the mind to focus on the movement of the stomach, we can develop greater concentration and mental clarity. This can help with tasks that require sustained attention and focus, such as studying or working on a project.
- **Reduced Stress and Anxiety:** Mindfulness meditation has been shown to be an effective tool for reducing stress and anxiety. By becoming more aware of our thoughts and feelings, and developing a non-judgmental attitude towards them, we can learn to manage stress and anxiety more effectively.

- **Improved Emotional Regulation:** Mindfulness meditation can also help improve emotional regulation. By learning to observe our thoughts and feelings without reacting to them, we can develop greater emotional resilience and stability.
- **Better Sleep:** Regular mindfulness practice has been shown to improve sleep quality and reduce insomnia. By calming the mind and reducing stress and anxiety, we can achieve a restful and rejuvenating sleep.
- **Greater Self-awareness:** Mindfulness meditation can help us develop a deeper understanding of ourselves and our inner experiences. By observing our thoughts, feelings, and bodily sensations, we can gain insights into our patterns of behavior and beliefs, and make positive changes in our lives.

2. **Walking Meditation:** Walking meditation is a mindfulness practice that involves paying close attention to the physical sensation of walking. It is a popular form of mindfulness practice that can be done indoors or outdoors, and can be done alone or with a group. The practice of walking meditation is simple. Start by finding a quiet and peaceful place where you can walk without interruption. Stand still and take a few deep breaths, focusing your attention on your breath as it moves in and out of your body. Begin walking slowly, paying close attention to the sensation of each foot as it touches the ground. Focus your attention on the movement of your body as you walk, the shifting of your weight from one foot to the other, and the sensation of your feet lifting and lowering. As you walk, try to remain present and mindful of your

surroundings. Notice the sights, sounds, and smells around you without becoming lost in thought. If your mind starts to wander, simply notice the thought and gently bring your attention back to the physical sensation of walking.

Exercise:

1. Find a quiet and peaceful place where you can walk without interruption.
2. Begin by standing still, with your feet shoulder-width apart and your arms relaxed at your sides. Take a few deep breaths and focus your attention on your body, starting from the head and moving down to the toes. Then, shift your focus and move up from the toes back to the head in a mindful way.
3. Slowly lift your left foot and take a step forward. As you do this, focus your attention on the movement of your foot and the sensations in your body.
4. Place your left foot on the ground and shift your weight onto it. Again, pay attention to the sensations in your body as you do this.
5. Slowly lift your right foot and take a step forward. Once again, focus your attention on the movement of your foot and the sensations in your body.
6. Place your right foot on the ground and shift your weight onto it. As before, pay attention to the sensations in your body.
7. Repeat steps 3-6, taking 10–12 steps forward and then stopping to stand still for a moment. Then, turn around slowly and begin walking back in the

opposite direction. Keep your attention focused on the movement of your body and the sensations you experience throughout the meditation.

8. Repeat this process for 4-6 rounds of walking meditation each day.

Walking meditation can be a great way to incorporate mindfulness into your daily routine and can be done for any length of time. It's possible to practice walking meditation at an even slower pace. It can be a refreshing break from sitting meditation and can help bring mindfulness to your body and movement. With regular practice, walking meditation can help increase your awareness and presence in daily life, allowing you to be more mindful and attentive in all aspects of your life.

3. **Sitting Meditation:** Sitting meditation is a mindfulness practice that involves sitting in a comfortable position, often with legs crossed and hands resting on the knees, and focusing attention on the present moment. Sitting meditation is commonly practiced in Buddhist traditions, but it can also be found in other spiritual or secular contexts. The goal of sitting meditation is to develop a clear and focused mind, cultivate inner calmness, and increase self-awareness. During the practice, the meditator pays close attention to their breath and physical sensations while acknowledging and letting go of any distracting thoughts or emotions that arise. To begin a sitting meditation practice, find a quiet and comfortable place to sit with your back straight and your eyes closed or partially closed. Set a timer for a desired length of time, starting with just a few minutes and gradually

increasing the duration over time. Begin by taking a few deep breaths to relax your body and bring your attention to the present moment. Then, focus on your breath and the sensation of air moving in and out of your body. Observe the rise and fall of your stomach. As you continue to focus on the movement of your stomach, you may notice distracting thoughts or emotions arising. Simply acknowledge them and let them go, returning your attention to observing your stomach's movement. You may find it helpful to use a mantra or a word to bring your focus back to the present moment.

Exercise:

1. Find a quiet and comfortable place to sit with a straight back.
2. Close your eyes or lower your gaze, and take a few deep breaths to relax your body.
3. Bring your attention to your breath and focus on the sensation of air moving in and out of your nostrils or on the rise and fall of your abdomen with each breath.
4. If your mind begins to wander, gently bring your attention back to your breath.
5. As you sit, notice any sensations, emotions, or thoughts that arise, but try not to get caught up in them. Simply observe them and let them pass.
6. Practice for a set amount of time, such as 10–20 minutes, or longer if you prefer.
7. When you're finished, take a few deep breaths and slowly open your eyes. Take a moment to notice how you feel before standing up and resuming your activities.

Sitting meditation can be practiced daily, either alone or in a group setting. Regular practice has been shown to improve focus, reduce stress, and promote overall well-being.

4. **Daily Activities Mindfulness:** The practice of mindfulness involves being fully present and aware of each moment and activity rather than being distracted or caught up in thoughts and worries about the past or future. All activities can be seen as opportunities to cultivate mindfulness and awareness. Here are some examples of daily activities that can be transformed into mindfulness practices:

   • **Eating:** Pay close attention to the food you are eating, the sensations in your mouth, and the act of chewing and swallowing. Also, be aware of the source of the food, how it was prepared, and the impact of your choices on the environment and other beings.
   • **Brushing Teeth:** Pay attention to the sensation of the toothbrush on the teeth, the taste of the toothpaste, and the sound of brushing.
   • **Driving:** Stay focused on the road, observe your surroundings, and stay present in the moment.
   • **Washing Dishes:** Focus on the sensation of water and soap on your hands, the texture of the dishes, and the sound of water running.
   • **Walking:** Pay attention to the sensations in your feet, legs, and body as you move, as well as the sights, sounds, and smells around you. Also, be aware of your breath and mental state as you walk.

- **Working:** Be fully engaged in your work rather than distracted or daydreaming, and be aware of your intentions and mental states as you work, as well as the impact of your work on others.
- **Communicating:** Being fully present and attentive to the person you are speaking with, rather than distracted or preoccupied, and also being aware of your own thoughts and emotions as well as the impact of your words on others

These are just a few examples of how mindfulness can be incorporated into daily activities. The key is to bring full attention and awareness to whatever you are doing in the present moment. The benefits of practicing mindfulness in all activities are numerous. It can deepen our understanding of ourselves and others and help us cultivate greater compassion and kindness toward ourselves and others.

The Power of Meditation

These days, life presents various challenges that affect our personal lives, work, and health. These challenges include relationship issues, family conflicts, financial struggles, personal crises, job-related stress, difficult colleagues, work-life balance, and health problems. Coping with these challenges can be emotionally draining, leading to stress, anxiety, and depression. In this book, my goal is not to achieve enlightenment but to offer practical mindfulness training from meditation practice to help navigate life's difficulties and move forward with greater ease. Could I share a story with you about someone who was able to overcome a difficult situation by practicing meditation? It's a really inspiring story that shows the power of mindfulness to help us navigate through challenging times. During my college years in Thailand, I participated in a profound eight-day meditation retreat. While there, I crossed paths with a successful and wealthy woman who seemed to be facing a personal challenge. As it turned out, she had recently gone through a divorce and was feeling quite depressed. She had come to the retreat in hopes of finding some peace of mind through meditation. On the last day of the retreat, she shared her story with the group, saying that she had always been successful in every aspect of her life, including education, career, and belonging to a wealthy family. She had never faced any disappointments or failures until she experienced the most challenging time of her life: her marriage came to an end in a divorce, leaving her feeling defeated and lost. She shared that meditation had helped her understand the importance of accepting her situation and letting go of the past to move forward. Through this practice, she learned that she couldn't control everything or anyone around her, but she could control her mind and how she responded to her circumstances. By training her mind to accept the situation and find ways to move forward, she was able to overcome this difficult time. The experience she shared illustrates how meditation can assist us in finding clarity and inner peace during challenging times and enable us to adjust to new circumstances with a stronger sense of balance and serenity.

According to Buddhism, suffering arises from attachment to things that are impermanent, and meditation practice can help us release these attachments and gain deeper insights into the nature of reality. Through mindfulness meditation, we can learn to observe our thoughts and emotions without judgment and cultivate inner calm and self-compassion. This can be a powerful tool for coping with the challenges we face in life. In the upcoming chapters, we will delve into the fascinating history of Buddhism, exploring its origins and development over time. We will examine the life of the Buddha, one of the most important figures in the Buddhist tradition. Additionally, we will explore the intersections between Buddhism and science, examining the ways in which modern scientific research has shed new light on Buddhist principles and practices and vice versa. From the benefits of meditation for mental and physical health to the ways in which neuroscience is uncovering the mechanisms underlying Buddhist insights, we will explore the exciting connections between these two fields of study.

8

THE HISTORY OF BUDDHISM

S O FAR, we have explored Buddhism's teachings and practices. Learning about how Buddhism originated and spread worldwide is valuable in understanding its global journey as a religion. It adapted to diverse cultures, enriching them along the way. The spread of Buddhism also reveals the connections between civilizations. Moreover, lessons from its dissemination have present-day applications in fostering interfaith dialogue and cultural exchange. Ultimately, studying Buddhism's journey enhances our understanding of its historical significance, cultural influence, and relevance in our interconnected world. This chapter will provide you with deeper insights into the origins of Buddhism.

From the Buddha to the Spread of Buddhism

The history of Buddhism dates back over 2,500 years to ancient India, where it originated with the life and teachings of Siddhartha Gautama, known as the Buddha. Siddhartha was born in the 5th century BCE into a royal family in what is now Nepal. Despite his privileged upbringing, he became deeply aware of the suffering and impermanence of human existence. Seeking answers to the universal questions of suffering, the nature of reality, and the path to liberation, he renounced his royal status and embarked on a spiritual quest. After years of intense meditation and self-discovery, he attained enlightenment under a Bodhi tree in Bodh Gaya, India. From that moment on, he became the Buddha, or "the awakened one." The Buddha spent the remaining years of his life traveling across India, teaching his profound insights and principles to all who would listen. His teachings, known as the Dharma, emphasized the Four Noble Truths: the truth of suffering, the truth of the cause of suffering, the truth of the cessation of suffering, and the truth of the path leading to the cessation of suffering. The Buddha's teachings resonated with people from all walks of life. After the Buddha's passing, his teachings were orally transmitted and eventually recorded in Buddhist scriptures. These texts became the primary source of Buddhist teachings and formed the basis for the development of various Buddhist schools and traditions.

Buddhism began to spread in Asia shortly after the death of the Buddha in the 5th century BCE. Initially, Buddhism gained popularity in India, the birthplace of the religion, and gradually expanded its influence beyond its homeland. The support of rulers and emperors played a crucial role in spreading Buddhism. Emperor Ashoka of the Mauryan Empire in India played a crucial role in promoting Buddhism. He embraced the teachings of the Buddha and actively supported the dissemination of Buddhist principles throughout his empire. Ashoka's efforts, including the erection of pillars and inscriptions, helped to establish Buddhism as a prominent religion in ancient India. Buddhism also spread through trade routes that connected different regions of Asia. The Silk Road, a vast network of trade routes stretching from China to the Mediterranean, facilitated the exchange of goods, ideas, and religious beliefs. Buddhist monks and merchants traveling along these routes carried Buddhist teachings to Central Asia, China, and beyond.

In Central Asia, the Kushan Empire became a significant center for the transmission of Buddhism. The Kushan rulers actively supported and patronized the religion. Buddhist monasteries and art flourished under their rule, contributing to the spread of Buddhism in the region. In China, Buddhism arrived during the Han Dynasty (206 BCE–220 CE) and gradually gained followers. Buddhist scriptures were translated into Chinese, making the teachings accessible to a wider audience. Buddhism in China merged with existing cultural and religious practices, giving rise to distinct Chinese Buddhist traditions. Buddhism also reached Southeast Asia through maritime trade routes and cultural interactions. It found its way to countries such as Myanmar (Burma), Thailand, Cambodia, and Laos. In these regions, Buddhism interacted with indigenous beliefs and practices, leading to the development of unique forms of Buddhism. Japan's encounter with Buddhism occurred in the 6th century CE, primarily through cultural exchanges with China and Korea. Buddhism gained royal patronage and became deeply ingrained in Japanese society. Various Buddhist sects and schools emerged, each with its own distinct teachings and practices. Buddhism spread in ancient Asia through trade, patronage, scripture translation, and cultural exchanges. The adaptability of Buddhism to local customs and beliefs played a significant role in its acceptance and integration into different Asian societies. Over time, Buddhism became a major religion in many Asian countries, contributing to the region's rich cultural heritage.

Buddhism has had a significant impact on the cultures and societies it has encountered. It spread to various parts of Asia, where it integrated with local beliefs and customs. Buddhist art, architecture, literature, and philosophy flourished, leaving a lasting imprint on these civilizations. Nowadays, Buddhism has become a global religion with followers and practitioners across the world. Its teachings on mindfulness, compassion, and wisdom continue to inspire people to seek inner peace, live ethically, and cultivate a deeper understanding of the nature of existence. The rich history of Buddhism reflects its resilience, adaptability, and enduring appeal as a path towards personal transformation and spiritual awakening. Additionally, Buddhism emphasizes the concept of impermanence, teaching that all conditioned phenomena are subject to change. It challenges the notion of a permanent and independent self, emphasizing the idea of no self and the interconnectedness of all things. Meditation is a fundamental practice in Buddhism. It plays a crucial role in developing mindfulness, concentration, and insight. It is employed to cultivate inner awareness and achieve a deeper understanding of reality.

Three Main Types of Buddhism

Buddhism is commonly categorized into three major branches: Theravada, Mahayana, and Vajrayana. Each branch has its own unique interpretations, practices, rituals, and scriptures while sharing a common aim of attaining enlightenment and liberation from suffering.

- **Theravada Buddhism** is the oldest surviving branch of Buddhism. It is predominantly practiced in Sri Lanka, Myanmar (Burma), Thailand, Laos, Cambodia, and parts of Vietnam. Theravada focuses on the original teachings of the Buddha and emphasizes meditation and personal liberation through individual effort.

- **Mahayana Buddhism** is widely practiced in East Asia, including China, Japan, Korea, Vietnam, and Tibet. Mahayana emphasizes compassion and the aspiration to attain enlightenment not only for oneself but also for the benefit of all beings. It places importance on bodhisattvas—enlightened beings who delay their own liberation to assist others.
- **Vajrayana Buddhism** is practiced primarily in the Himalayan regions, including Tibet, Nepal, Bhutan, and parts of Mongolia. It incorporates elements of Mahayana Buddhism along with indigenous Tibetan practices. Vajrayana places emphasis on advanced meditation techniques, rituals, mantras, and the use of symbols and mandalas to facilitate spiritual transformation.

In Thailand, Theravada Buddhism is officially recognized as the country's religion and has a substantial impact on Thai culture, traditions, and the daily lives of its people. Thai Buddhists engage in various practices, such as offering food to monks, giving alms, participating in meditation retreats, chanting, and making offerings at temples. These practices are regarded as ways to accumulate merit and foster spiritual growth. Hence, all the information contained within this book is grounded in the principles and teachings of Theravada Buddhism.

Buddhism Unique Characteristics

Buddhism possesses several unique characteristics that differentiate it from other religions. First and foremost,

Buddhism is a **non-theistic religion**, meaning it does not believe in a personal creator deity or supreme being. Instead, Buddhism emphasizes understanding and addressing the nature of suffering, its causes, and the path to liberation through individual effort and self-transformation. Unlike religions that rely on a higher power for salvation, Buddhism encourages practitioners to seek answers and insights within themselves. It teaches that each individual has the potential to cultivate wisdom, compassion, and inner peace through practices such as meditation, mindfulness, and ethical living. The absence of a personal deity in Buddhism allows for a more direct and personal approach to spirituality. Followers are encouraged to rely on their own experiences, critical thinking, and self-reflection to comprehend the nature of reality and their place within it. Moreover, Buddhism embraces an inclusive and open-minded perspective due to its non-theistic nature. It welcomes individuals from various religious backgrounds and encourages dialogue, exploration, and continuous learning rather than imposing dogma or rigid beliefs. This openness provides space for personal growth and spiritual development through self-discovery, questioning, and introspection.

Additionally, Buddhism places significant emphasis on **self-discovery** as a core aspect of its teachings. It invites individuals to embark on a journey of exploration, delving into their own experiences, insights, and inner wisdom. Rather than relying solely on external authority or scripture, Buddhism highlights personal responsibility and the cultivation of self-awareness. Through practices such as meditation, mindfulness, and self-reflection, individuals deepen their understanding of themselves and the nature of reality. Buddhism recognizes that genuine insight and transformation come from direct personal experience and introspection. It encourages individuals to question their beliefs, assumptions, and attachments, fostering autonomy and independent thinking. By engaging in self-discovery, practitioners develop a deeper connection with their inner truth and authenticity. They learn to trust their own experiences and insights, cultivating greater self-awareness and self-reliance. This emphasis on self-discovery empowers individuals to actively participate in their spiritual journey, promoting personal growth and enabling them to navigate life with clarity and wisdom.

Furthermore, Buddhism incorporates concepts such as **reincarnation and karma**, suggesting that individuals undergo a cycle of rebirth based on their actions. This belief underscores the significance of ethical conduct and personal responsibility in shaping future lives. Buddhism also places considerable emphasis on mindfulness and meditation practices, which cultivate awareness, concentration, and insight. These practices are central to the Buddhist path and contribute to personal transformation and liberation. Moreover, Buddhism promotes compassion and loving-kindness towards all sentient beings, recognizing the interconnectedness of all life forms and encouraging the development of empathy and altruism.

Another aspect that sets Buddhism apart is its emphasis on reflecting the **laws of nature**. Buddhism teaches that its principles and teachings align with the natural laws that govern the universe. It encourages individuals to observe and understand these laws through personal experience and direct observation, rather than relying solely on faith or external authority. This approach, grounded in personal responsibility and individual exploration, allows practitioners to develop a deeper understanding of the natural order and their place within it. By reflecting the laws of nature, Buddhism offers a unique perspective on life, suffering, and the path to liberation. In summary, Buddhism's non-theistic nature, emphasis on self-discovery, inclusivity, personal responsibility, and reflection of natural laws distinguish it from many other religious traditions. Buddhism offers a distinct path to enlightenment that relies on personal experience, introspection, and the cultivation of wisdom, compassion, and self-awareness.

Buddhism also promotes the **Middle Way**, a balanced approach that avoids extremes and encourages moderation in life. The Buddha himself discovered this path, finding that neither indulgence nor asceticism led to true happiness or spiritual awakening. The Middle Way offers valuable guidance in various areas of life, helping individuals navigate them with wisdom and balance. Here are some key areas where the Middle Way can be applied in practical terms:

- **Ethics:** The Middle Way guides ethical conduct, encouraging individuals to avoid extreme behavior. It advocates for a moral path that steers clear of excessive indulgence and harmful actions, as well as extreme self-denial or asceticism. By following ethical principles with moderation and mindfulness, one cultivates virtuous behavior that benefits oneself and others.

- **Mindfulness and Meditation:** The Middle Way is reflected in the practice of mindfulness and meditation. It encourages individuals to find a balanced approach to their meditation practice, avoiding both laziness and excessive striving. Practitioners are encouraged to observe thoughts and emotions without getting caught up in them, fostering a balanced and focused state of awareness.

- **Views and Beliefs:** The Middle Way influences the development of one's views and beliefs. It encourages practitioners to embrace an open-minded and nondogmatic attitude, avoiding clinging to fixed ideas or rigid doctrines. The Middle Way invites critical thinking, self-inquiry, and the ability to consider different perspectives, fostering a more inclusive and flexible approach to understanding the nature of reality.

- **Lifestyle and Material Possessions:** The Middle Way offers guidance on one's relationship with material possessions and lifestyle choices. It encourages individuals to neither be excessively attached to material wealth and pleasures nor to renounce them entirely. The Middle Way promotes a balanced approach, appreciating and using material resources mindfully while also recognizing their impermanence and not becoming enslaved by them.
- **Emotions and Mental States:** The Middle Way applies to managing emotions and mental states. It encourages individuals to find a middle ground between emotional suppression and unchecked indulgence. By cultivating equanimity, practitioners can acknowledge and accept their emotions without being overwhelmed by them. They seek a balanced state of mind, free from the extremes of craving, aversion, and delusion.

By embracing the Middle Way across these various aspects of life, individuals can cultivate a balanced and harmonious existence. It encourages finding a middle ground that avoids extremes and promotes well-being, wisdom, and compassionate action. The Middle Way serves as a practical guide for navigating life's challenges, fostering personal growth, and nurturing a sense of interconnectedness with all beings.

Buddhism is a deep and meaningful spiritual tradition that started long ago in India. It developed to help people find freedom from suffering and discover enlightenment. Buddhism teaches important ideas like the Four Noble Truths and the Noble Eightfold Path, which focus on gaining wisdom, being ethical, and practicing meditation. There are different kinds of Buddhism, each with its own unique teachings and practices. Whether it's Theravada, Mahayana, or Vajrayana, Buddhism inspires millions of people worldwide to seek inner peace, wisdom, and freedom. Its teachings about human life and its emphasis on compassion make Buddhism a timeless and universal path to awakening. The upcoming chapter will explore the relationship between Buddhism and science, examining their correlations and potential intersections.

9

BUDDHISM AND SCIENCE

I N THE previous chapter, we explored the origins of Buddhism. Now, in this chapter, we will dive deeper into the fascinating interplay between Buddhist beliefs and scientific principles. We will examine how these two domains of knowledge can inform and complement each other, offering valuable insights into the nature of reality, the mind, and our place in the world. By exploring the intersections between Buddhism and science, we can expand our understanding and cultivate a more holistic perspective on life and existence.

Buddhism-Science Commonality

Buddhist philosophy and science share a common ground in their approach to understanding the nature of reality. Both seek to investigate the fundamental nature of existence and the interconnectedness of all phenomena. Buddhism encourages inquiry, critical thinking, and direct experience, similar to the scientific method. The Buddhist concept of impermanence aligns with scientific findings on the ever-changing nature of the universe. Moreover, mindfulness practices advocated in Buddhism have been scientifically studied and shown to have numerous benefits for mental well-being. While Buddhism and science may differ in their methodologies and areas of focus, they can mutually enrich our understanding of the world and offer complementary perspectives on the nature of existence. Buddhism represents a distinctive synthesis of speculative and scientific philosophy, presenting a system of thought that places emphasis on rational and psychological aspects while de-emphasizing the mystical and mythological. While Buddhism upholds the scientific method and pursues it with unwavering dedication, it surpasses the limitations of science by delving into realms that science cannot fully explore. One of the core characteristics of Buddhism is the cultivation of a skeptical mindset, where propositions are scrutinized and accepted only upon careful examination of evidence. While Buddhism can be regarded as a science of the mind, it should not be confined to that domain alone. Both Buddhism and science share an empirical approach rooted in skepticism and the examination of evidence. The insights offered by Buddhist thought challenge scientists to critically assess their methodologies, question their logical constructs, and reexamine their assumptions. The engagement between Buddhism and science creates a fruitful dialogue, as the scientific community benefits from the introspective and contemplative techniques developed within Buddhism. Buddhist perspectives prompt scientists to consider the subjective dimensions of human experience and explore the potential limitations of purely objective methodologies. In turn, scientists' inquiries and findings invite Buddhists to scrutinize their own concepts, theories, and practices, fostering a reciprocal exchange of ideas.

This ongoing interaction between Buddhism and science fuels mutual enrichment as both disciplines strive to expand our understanding of the world and our place within it. It serves as a reminder that while Buddhism embraces empirical investigation and rational analysis, it also encompasses aspects that transcend the boundaries of conventional scientific inquiry. By recognizing the contributions and limitations of each domain, Buddhism and science can collectively advance our comprehension of reality and contribute to the betterment of humanity. Science and Buddhism share a common emphasis on the importance of examining and evaluating evidence before drawing conclusions. In the scientific method, researchers gather data through experimentation and observation, and then analyze and interpret the data to develop theories or explanations for natural phenomena. In Buddhism, practitioners are taught to be skeptical and to examine evidence before accepting any proposition or belief. Both science and Buddhism recognize the importance of objectivity in evaluating evidence. Scientists strive to minimize bias and subjectivity in their research by using controls and double-blind studies and replicating experiments to confirm findings. Similarly, Buddhist practitioners seek to develop a clear and objective awareness of their own thoughts, emotions, and sensations in order to better understand the nature of reality. Furthermore, both science and Buddhism emphasize the importance of ongoing inquiry and the revision of beliefs in light of new evidence. In science, new discoveries or data can challenge existing theories, leading to the development of new or modified theories. In Buddhism, practitioners are encouraged to continually examine their own beliefs and perceptions, recognizing that they are subject to change as their understanding deepens. Overall, the emphasis on evidence and inquiry in both science and Buddhism highlights the value of a rational and critical approach to understanding the world and ourselves. By cultivating an attitude of skepticism, objectivity, and openness to new evidence, we can gain a deeper and more accurate understanding of the nature of reality.

Buddhist concepts and teachings often emphasize subjective experiences, inner transformation, and the nature of the mind. While they may not align with scientific principles in their entirety, there are certain aspects that can be related to scientific understanding. Here are some key concepts in Buddhism that can be seen in relation to scientific principles:

- **Impermanence:** The Buddhist concept of impermanence teaches us that everything in the world is constantly changing and nothing remains the same. This idea aligns with the *Scientific Principle of Entropy*, which states that all systems tend to move towards disorder over time. Both concepts share similarities and differences in their understanding of change and the nature of phenomena. In common, both impermanence and the law of entropy recognize that nothing in the world remains fixed or permanent. They emphasize that all things are subject to constant change and fluctuation. Impermanence in Buddhism teaches us to let go of attachments and accept the transient nature of all phenomena, while the law of entropy explains that all systems tend to move towards greater disorder over time unless energy is input to counteract this tendency. However, there are also differences between impermanence and the law of entropy. Impermanence is a philosophical concept rooted in the Buddhist understanding of existence, encompassing physical objects, emotions, thoughts, and the self. It emphasizes the impermanence of all phenomena and the suffering that arises from clinging to what is inherently changing. On the other hand, the law of entropy is a scientific principle derived from the second law of thermodynamics, specifically describing the tendency of closed systems to move towards increased disorder or randomness. While both impermanence and the law of entropy recognize the dynamic nature of reality, they differ in scope and application. Impermanence applies to all aspects of existence and serves as a foundation for Buddhist teachings on detachment and non-attachment. The law of entropy, on the other hand, is a specific principle in thermodynamics that describes the behavior of physical systems. In summary, impermanence and the law of entropy both highlight the transient nature of phenomena and the inevitability of change. They provide valuable insights into the nature of reality from different perspectives: one philosophical and spiritual, and the other scientific. While they share a common recognition of impermanence, they differ in their scope and application. Understanding and contemplating these concepts can provide a broader perspective on the nature of existence and deepen our appreciation for the dynamic and ever-changing world we inhabit.

- **Mindfulness:** Mindfulness, a key practice in Buddhism, involves paying attention to the present moment with non-judgmental awareness. This concept can be related to the *Scientific Principle of Attentional Control*, which suggests that the ability to focus one's attention can have significant benefits for mental health and cognitive functioning. The connection between mindfulness and attentional control lies in their shared emphasis on training and refining attention. Through mindfulness practice, individuals develop the capacity to direct and sustain their attention in the present moment, cultivating a heightened awareness of their inner and outer experiences. Scientific research has shown that mindfulness training can enhance attentional control. Regular mindfulness practice has been found to improve attentional focus, increase cognitive flexibility, and enhance the ability to disengage from distracting thoughts and stimuli. Mindfulness training improves attentional control for intentional focus, freeing individuals from automatic and reactive thoughts. This can lead to improved cognitive performance, emotional regulation, and overall well-being. While mindfulness and attentional control are not identical, they share a common objective of honing attentional abilities. The scientific understanding of attentional control helps validate and provide insights into the benefits of mindfulness practice. By integrating mindfulness techniques into scientific studies, researchers have been able to investigate the effects of mindfulness on attentional processes, brain activity, and overall mental functioning. This intersection of Buddhism and science contributes to a deeper understanding of the potential benefits of mindfulness and its relationship to attentional control. In summary, mindfulness practice in Buddhism and the scientific principle of attentional control both recognize the importance of training and regulating attention. They offer complementary perspectives on how attention can be harnessed and developed, leading to improved cognitive functioning and greater self-awareness.

- **Interconnectedness:** The Buddhist concept of interconnectedness, or the idea that all things are connected and depend on one another, can be related to the *Scientific Principle of Systems Theory*, which looks at how complex systems are made up of interconnected parts. Interconnectedness in Buddhism highlights the notion that everything in the world is interconnected and interdependent. It recognizes that no phenomenon exists in isolation and that all things arise from and depend on multiple causes and conditions. This concept extends beyond individuals and encompasses the interdependence of all living beings and the natural world. Systems theory, in science, studies the interconnectedness and interdependencies within complex systems. It recognizes that systems are composed of multiple interconnected parts that interact and influence each other. It emphasizes understanding the relationships, feedback loops, and dynamic interactions that shape the behavior and functioning of systems. The connection between interconnectedness and systems theory lies in their shared emphasis on recognizing the interdependencies and relationships within a larger whole. Both highlight that individual components or entities cannot be fully understood in isolation but rather need to be studied within the context of their relationships and interactions with other elements. Systems theory provides a scientific framework for studying the interconnectedness that Buddhism has long recognized. It helps researchers analyze complex phenomena by considering the relationships, interdependencies, and feedback loops that exist within systems. By applying systems thinking to various fields of study, including ecology, sociology, and psychology, scientists gain insights into how different elements influence and depend on each other. This aligns with the Buddhist understanding that our actions, thoughts, and emotions are not isolated occurrences but interconnected with the larger web of existence. Moreover, the recognition of interconnectedness in both Buddhism and systems theory can foster a sense of responsibility and ethical consideration. Understanding the interdependencies between individuals and the environment can promote a more holistic and sustainable approach to human interactions with the natural world. In summary, the Buddhist concept of interconnectedness and the scientific principle of systems theory both emphasize the recognition of interdependencies and relationships within complex systems. They provide valuable insights into the interconnected nature of reality and offer frameworks for studying and understanding the dynamic interactions that shape our world.

- **Karma:** The Buddhist concept of karma, or the idea that actions have consequences that affect future outcomes, can be related to the *Scientific Principle of Cause and Effect*, which suggests that all events have a cause and an effect. It suggests that our actions, intentions, and thoughts have consequences that shape our present and future experiences. Positive actions lead to positive outcomes, while negative actions result in negative consequences. Karma is not seen as a form of cosmic justice or punishment but rather as a natural law that operates in accordance with cause and effect. The scientific principle of

THE BUDDHA SAID WHAT?!

cause and effect is a fundamental concept in various scientific disciplines. It states that every action has a corresponding reaction or consequence. In scientific inquiry, researchers strive to identify and understand the causal relationships between different phenomena. They investigate how specific causes lead to particular effects and seek to establish reliable patterns and mechanisms of causation. The connection between the concept of karma and the scientific principle of cause and effect lies in their shared recognition of the relationship between actions and outcomes. Both Buddhism and science acknowledge the influence of past actions on present experiences and recognize that our current actions shape our future experiences. Scientific studies in fields such as psychology, sociology, and neuroscience have explored the causal links between actions and behaviors and their consequences for individual well-being and social dynamics. This research aligns with the understanding in Buddhism that our actions have far-reaching implications for ourselves and others. Furthermore, both karma and the scientific principle of cause and effect emphasize personal responsibility and the power of intentional action. They highlight that we have agency in shaping our experiences and outcomes through our choices and behaviors. This recognition can foster a sense of accountability and encourage individuals to make conscious, skillful choices that lead to positive results. While karma and the scientific principle of cause and effect share similarities in recognizing the relationship between actions and consequences, it's important to note that their perspectives and frameworks differ.

Karma encompasses not only observable cause-and-effect relationships but also mental intentions and the influence of past lives. It addresses the broader spiritual and ethical dimensions of human existence beyond the scope of scientific inquiry. In conclusion, the concept of karma in Buddhism and the scientific principle of cause and effect both highlight the relationship between actions and their consequences. They emphasize personal responsibility, the power of intention, and the understanding that our choices and behaviors have a significant impact on our lives and the world around us.

• **Emptiness:** The Buddhist concept of emptiness, or the idea that all things lack inherent existence, can be related to the *Scientific Principle of Quantum Mechanics*, which suggests that subatomic particles exist in a state of probability until they are observed or measured. In Buddhism, emptiness refers to the understanding that all phenomena lack inherent or independent existence. It teaches that everything is interdependent and interconnected, and there is no fixed or permanent essence or self. Emptiness is not a state of nothingness but rather a recognition that things are empty of their inherent, separate existence and are instead interrelated and interdependent. Quantum mechanics, a branch of physics, is a scientific theory that describes the behavior of particles and energy at the subatomic level. It introduces concepts such as wave-particle duality and uncertainty, which challenge classical notions of determinism and solid, independent entities. Quantum mechanics reveals that particles can exist in multiple states simultaneously and that observation and measurement can influence

THE BUDDHA SAID WHAT?!

their behavior. The connection between emptiness and quantum mechanics lies in their shared exploration of the nature of reality and the limitations of conventional, dualistic thinking. Both challenge the notion of a fixed, independently existing reality and point to the dynamic, interconnected nature of existence. Quantum mechanics shows that at the subatomic level, particles can exist in a superposition of states until they are observed or measured, indicating the inseparability of the observer and the observed. This aligns with the Buddhist view that phenomena arise in dependence on perception and consciousness. Furthermore, the uncertainty principle in quantum mechanics asserts that there are inherent limits to the precision with which certain pairs of physical properties can be simultaneously measured. This reflects the notion of emptiness in Buddhism, as it suggests that phenomena lack fixed, determinate properties and that our attempts to grasp or define them are inherently limited. While the concept of emptiness in Buddhism and the principles of quantum mechanics share similarities in questioning the nature of reality and the limitations of our understanding, it is important to note that they operate in different domains. Buddhism explores the existential and philosophical dimensions of emptiness, addressing the nature of suffering and the path to liberation. Quantum mechanics, on the other hand, is a scientific framework that provides mathematical models to describe the behavior of particles and energy. In conclusion, the concept of emptiness in Buddhism and the scientific principle of quantum mechanics both challenge conventional notions of fixed, independent reality. They invite us to examine the interconnected and dynamic nature of existence. While they approach the topic from different perspectives, they offer insights that can expand our understanding of the nature of reality and our place within it.

* **Reality:** Buddhism teaches that our perceptions of reality are subjective and depend on our individual experiences and interpretations. Similarly, *Einstein's Theory of Relativity* states that time and space are relative to the observer's frame of reference. The theory of relativity is based on two main ideas: the principle of relativity and the constancy of the speed of light. The principle of relativity states that the laws of physics are the same for all observers, regardless of their relative motion. This means that there is no absolute frame of reference in the universe and that all motion must be measured relative to other objects. The constancy of the speed of light is the second main idea of the theory of relativity. According to this principle, the speed of light in a vacuum is always constant, regardless of the motion of the observer or the source of the light. This means that time and space must be relative and that they can change depending on the observer's frame of reference. One of the key predictions of the theory of relativity is that time can be affected by gravity. This was confirmed by the observation of gravitational time dilation, which occurs when time appears to slow down in a strong gravitational field. Another prediction of the theory of relativity is the phenomenon of gravitational lensing, in which light is bent by the curvature of space-time near a massive object. The theory of

relativity has also had significant implications for our understanding of the structure and evolution of the universe. It predicts that the universe is expanding and that the rate of expansion is accelerating. This prediction was confirmed by observations of distant supernovae in the late 1990s and has led to the development of the concept of dark energy, which is thought to be driving the accelerating expansion of the universe. The theory of relativity is one of the most important scientific theories ever developed and has had a profound impact on our understanding of the nature of space, time, and the universe as a whole. Buddhism teaches that our perceptions of reality are subjective and depend on our individual experiences and interpretations. This is similar to the concept of relativity in physics, as it suggests that reality is not absolute but rather relative to the observer's frame of reference. One of the key ideas of relativity is that there is no such thing as absolute rest or absolute motion. Instead, all motion is relative to the observer's frame of reference. This means that different observers can experience different measurements of space and time depending on their relative speeds and positions. Similarly, Buddhism teaches that our perceptions of reality are shaped by our own subjective experiences and interpretations. Two people can observe the same event and come away with completely different understandings of what happened, based on their own biases and perspectives. Therefore, in Buddhism, it is essential to cultivate mindfulness and awareness of our own subjective perceptions in order to gain a clearer understanding of reality. Overall, the concept of relativity in physics and the teachings of Buddhism share a fundamental idea: reality is not absolute but rather relative to the observer's frame of reference or subjective experiences. Both encourage us to be aware of our own perceptions and biases in order to gain a deeper understanding of the world around us.

• **Reincarnation:** The Buddhist belief in reincarnation, where consciousness or energy is thought to continue after death but in a new form or body, can be related to *the Law of Conservation of Energy*, which states that energy cannot be created or destroyed, only transformed from one form to another. This law is closely related to the concept of the conservation of mass, which states that mass cannot be created or destroyed, only transformed. While this scientific law may not directly correspond to every aspect of Buddhist teachings, it can provide a useful framework for understanding some of the fundamental concepts of Buddhism. This law implies that the total amount of energy within a closed system remains constant over time. Some individuals see a parallel between this law and the idea that the energy that comprises a person's being or consciousness could undergo a transformation rather than cease to exist upon death. Consequently, it is proposed that the energy that vitalizes an individual during their lifetime, encompassing their thoughts, emotions, and consciousness, may persist in some manner beyond physical death. This energy might then be transferred or transformed, giving rise to the concept of reincarnation. In Buddhism, the concept of energy conservation can be related to the idea of karma. Karma is the concept that every action we take has consequences, and those consequences are determined by the energy that we put into the action.

Just as energy cannot be created or destroyed, our actions and their consequences cannot be avoided or erased. This is why Buddhism teaches the importance of mindfulness and intention in our actions, as we must be aware of the energy that we are putting into the world and the consequences that will follow. The Law of Conservation of Energy and the concept of karma both teach us that our actions have a lasting impact on the world and that we must be mindful of the energy that we put into it. This can help us live more intentionally and compassionately, with a greater awareness of the consequences of our actions.

A Path of "Investigate before Believe"

Approaching any belief system, including Buddhism, with a healthy sense of skepticism and critical thinking is encouraged. Buddhism itself emphasizes the importance of personal investigation and direct experience rather than blind faith. It encourages individuals to question and examine its teachings before accepting them. In Buddhism, the emphasis is on personal exploration, self-reflection, and the development of insight through practice. It invites individuals to test the teachings in their own lives and see if they lead to greater understanding, inner peace, and transformation. This experiential approach allows individuals to verify the validity of Buddhist teachings based on their own direct experiences. It is important to note that not all aspects of Buddhism can be easily measured or proven through conventional scientific methods. Buddhism often deals with subjective experiences, the nature of the mind, and existential questions that go beyond the scope of empirical science. While scientific methods can provide valuable insights and correlations, they may not fully capture the depth and intricacies of spiritual experiences. Ultimately, the decision to believe or accept Buddhist teachings rests with the individual. Buddhism encourages open-mindedness, critical inquiry, and personal exploration. It invites individuals to examine the teachings, put them into practice, and assess their own experiences to determine their validity. This approach fosters a sense of personal responsibility and empowers individuals to develop their own understanding and insights.

In conclusion, Buddhism and science share important similarities. Buddhism's ideas about impermanence, mindfulness, interconnectedness, karma, emptiness, reality and reincarnation align with scientific principles. They both explore the ever-changing nature of the universe, interconnectedness in systems, and the impact of actions. Scientific research supports the benefits of mindfulness and meditation, which Buddhism emphasizes. The compatibility between Buddhism and science opens doors for collaboration and a holistic understanding of ourselves and the world. By embracing these shared principles, we can deepen our knowledge, improve well-being, and contribute to a better world. In the upcoming chapter, we will delve into the life and teachings of the Buddha, the enlightened one who discovered Buddhism and shared its profound teachings with people across the globe.

10

THE BUDDHA

S O FAR, I believe that you have gained valuable knowledge by exploring Buddhism and its teachings. To truly understand the importance of Buddhism, it is crucial to understand the life and teachings of the Buddha. By studying the wisdom and ideas of the individual who initiated this spiritual tradition, you can establish a personal connection with its essence and apply its teachings to your own life. Furthermore, delving into the historical and cultural context of the Buddha's era provides a broader understanding of how Buddhism has impacted different societies. By exploring the life of the Buddha, we recognize his significant contribution to humanity and the potential for personal growth and spiritual awakening that his teachings offer. This exploration not only enhances our spiritual journey but also fosters a deeper appreciation for the profound influence of Buddhism. In this chapter, we will explore the remarkable journey of the Buddha, from his upbringing as a prince in a sheltered palace to his profound encounter with the realities of human suffering and the impermanence of existence. These experiences led him to embark on a profound quest for truth, seeking answers to the fundamental questions of existence and the nature of suffering. This chapter will provide an understanding of the Buddha's life and the enduring impact of his message on individuals and societies throughout history. Through the exploration of the Buddha's path, we can discover profound insights and practical tools for personal growth, inner transformation, and the pursuit of genuine happiness and peace.

The Beginning of Buddha

The Buddha was born in the 5th century BCE into a royal family. His father, King Suddhodana, was the ruler of the Shakya kingdom, which was located in what is now modern-day Nepal. His mother, Queen Maya, was a princess from a neighboring kingdom. The Buddha's family gave him the name Siddhartha, which means "He Who Achieves His Goal", and his clan name was Gautama, which means "Descendant of Gotama." The name Gotama itself signifies "One Who Possesses The Most Light". King Suddhodana, the father of Siddhartha Gautama, was a powerful monarch who ruled over the Shakya kingdom in ancient India. He was admired for his wisdom, compassion, and leadership, earning the love and respect of his people. He was also a devout follower of Hinduism and believed in the importance of performing religious rituals and making offerings to the gods. Queen Maya, the wife of King Suddhodana and the mother of Siddhartha Gautama, had a profound dream of great significance before the birth of the Buddha. In the dream, she saw a white elephant with six tusks entering her womb from the right side, indicating that she would give birth to a son who would be a great spiritual leader. Soon after, she became pregnant. King Suddhodana sought advice from his advisors to interpret the dream. They concluded that it indicated that his son would either become a great king or a great spiritual leader. Siddhartha was born in Lumbini, a town situated between Kabilapat and Dhevataha in present-day Nepal. This happened while Queen Maya was on her way from the palace to her parents' home. Lumbini is a UNESCO World Heritage Site and is considered one of the most important pilgrimage sites for Buddhists around the world. After Siddhartha's birth, a hermit named Asita, who meditated in the Himmapan forest, predicted to King Suddhodana that his son possessed exceptional intelligence and the qualities of a remarkable individual. Asita prophesied that Siddhartha would renounce his privileged life and embark on a journey as an ascetic, seeking spiritual enlightenment. During this transformative journey, Siddhartha would achieve enlightenment as an Arahant, completely detached from all worldly desires and passions. Suddhodana was deeply disappointed with this prediction since he had anticipated that his son would become a great king. Asita's prophecy played a significant role in shaping the course of Siddhartha's life. It confirmed King Suddhodana's worst fears about his son, whom he hoped would one day become a powerful and successful ruler. The prophecy also affirmed Siddhartha's destiny, as he was destined to fulfill the prophecy and bring his teachings to the world.

As fate would have it, Queen Maya passed away just seven days after giving birth to Siddhartha. It is said that she departed from this world in the presence of her loved ones, experiencing no pain and finding peace. Although she did not live to see her son become the Buddha, her role in his life was significant. She provided him with a noble upbringing, and her passing served as a reminder of the impermanence of life, which became a central theme in Buddhist teachings. Queen Maya's death marked a significant turning point in Siddhartha's life. After the death of his mother, Siddhartha was raised by his maternal aunt, Mahaprajapati Gautami, who eventually married his father. She took on the role of his stepmother and continued to play a significant role in his upbringing, supporting his spiritual journey. As a father, Suddhodana had high expectations for his son. He hoped that his son would follow in his footsteps and become a great king who would rule the Shakya kingdom with wisdom and justice. To ensure that his son was prepared for his future role as king, Suddhodana arranged for Siddhartha to receive the best education possible. He hired the best teachers to teach him about politics, philosophy, and other important subjects. As a child, Siddhartha was raised in luxury and shielded from the realities of life outside the palace walls. King Suddhodana hoped his son would follow in his footsteps, so he did everything in his power to protect him from the harsh realities of the world and groom him for the role of a future king.

Escaping from Suffering

At the age of twenty-nine, Siddhartha ventured outside the palace and witnessed the suffering and poverty that existed beyond his sheltered life. This encounter with the harsh realities of the world exposed him to profound truths that became the driving force behind his quest for enlightenment. Some examples include:

- **Aging:** Siddhartha witnessed the inevitable process of aging as he encountered elderly individuals who were no longer in their prime physical condition. This confronted him with the transient nature of youth and beauty, highlighting the impermanence of life.

- **Sickness:** Siddhartha came face-to-face with people suffering from various illnesses. He observed the pain, discomfort, and vulnerability that accompanied physical ailments, recognizing the inherent suffering that arises from the body's fragility and susceptibility to disease.
- **Death:** The sight of a funeral procession and the realization that all beings are subject to death deeply impacted Siddhartha. He understood the universal nature of mortality and recognized the urgent need to find a way out of the cycle of birth, aging, sickness, and death.
- **Renunciation of Material Wealth:** Siddhartha encountered individuals living as ascetics who had renounced material possessions and pursued a simple, minimalist lifestyle. Their detachment from worldly desires and attachments demonstrated to him the potential freedom and contentment that could be achieved through a non-materialistic existence.
- **Wandering Ascetics:** Siddhartha met wandering ascetics who were diligently seeking spiritual truth and enlightenment through rigorous practices and self-discipline. Their unwavering commitment to their spiritual quest inspired him to embark on a similar path, abandoning his comfortable life in search of deeper understanding and liberation.

These encounters with the realities of life beyond the palace walls deeply affected Siddhartha, leading him to a profound realization of the impermanence, suffering, and unsatisfying nature of worldly existence. This realization ignited a strong determination within him to seek a path that would transcend these limitations and lead to lasting peace and liberation. Despite King Suddhodana's efforts to keep his son within the palace walls, the young prince could not escape the suffering he saw around him, and he became determined to find a way to end it. Siddhartha was not content with a life of luxury and materialism. He was deeply affected by witnessing the realities of aging, sickness, and death. The sight of an old man, a sick man, and a dead man opened his eyes to the universal nature of these experiences. It dawned on him that every person, regardless of their status or position, would eventually face these inevitable aspects of human existence. He became increasingly aware of the pain, sorrow, and impermanence that plagued humanity. This realization ignited his inner quest for answers and a way to alleviate suffering. Siddhartha eventually abandoned his comfortable life and embraced the life of a wandering ascetic with the goal of attaining spiritual enlightenment. In the end, Sudhodana's expectations for his son were far exceeded. He was extremely disheartened when Siddhartha left the palace to embark on this spiritual journey, as he had hoped for his son to return and assume his duties as a royal.

The Enlightenment

Once Siddhartha left the palace, he embraced a path of self-discovery and embarked on a transformative journey towards enlightenment. In his quest for ultimate truth, he explored various practices and disciplines from different spiritual traditions. Siddhartha sought guidance from renowned spiritual teachers, studying their teachings and methods. He practiced rigorous asceticism, subjecting himself to extreme self-discipline and deprivation in an effort to transcend the limitations of the human condition. For years, he engaged in intense meditation and severe self-mortification practices in the hope of transcending suffering. However, he soon realized that neither indulgence nor extreme self-mortification would lead him to the profound liberation he sought. Discarding these extremes, he adopted the Middle Way—a balanced approach that rejected both sensual indulgence and severe self-denial. One day, at the age of 35, while sitting under a bodhi tree in Bodh Gaya, he finally achieved enlightenment and became known as the Buddha, which means "the awakened one". In summary, Siddhartha employed various practices throughout his journey, encompassing renunciation, asceticism, the Middle Way, and meditation. These elements formed the foundation of his path towards enlightenment, ultimately leading him to a profound awakening and the emergence of the Buddha. Here are the key elements of his path and the approximate timeline:

- **Renunciation:** Siddhartha renounced his princely life, leaving behind the comforts of the palace in search of spiritual truth. This step marked the beginning of his journey towards enlightenment.
- **Ascetic Practices:** Initially, Siddhartha followed extreme ascetic practices, enduring severe self-mortification and deprivation. He pursued this path for around six years, seeking liberation through intense renunciation.
- **Middle Way:** Realizing that extreme asceticism did not lead to enlightenment, Siddhartha abandoned these practices. He adopted the Middle Way, a balanced approach that rejected both self-indulgence and self-mortification.
- **Meditation:** Siddhartha devoted himself to deep meditation, seeking profound states of concentration and mindfulness. He practiced meditation for an extended period, diligently exploring the nature of his mind and cultivating insight.
- **Enlightenment:** After years of dedicated effort, Siddhartha attained enlightenment under the famous

Bodhi tree in Bodh Gaya, India. It was during this intensive meditation that he experienced a profound awakening, gaining deep insights into the nature of reality and the causes of suffering. This transformative experience marked the culmination of his journey towards enlightenment. From that moment on, he became the Buddha—the Awakened One—and devoted the rest of his life to teaching others the path to liberation and the alleviation of suffering.

After his enlightenment, Buddha discovered the Four Noble Truths: the existence of suffering, its origin in attachment and craving, the possibility of overcoming suffering, and the Noble Eightfold Path as the means to achieve liberation. He spent the next forty-five years traveling throughout India, teaching others about his path to liberation and enlightenment, which included the Four Noble Truths. He attracted many followers, including monks and laypeople. He taught that the way to enlightenment was through self-awareness, compassion, and a deep understanding of the nature of reality. He also taught about karma, rebirth, and the nature of existence. The Buddha emphasized the significance of the Four Noble Truths and the Noble Eightfold Path as a means to overcome suffering and attain inner peace. His teachings placed a great emphasis on the power of mindfulness and compassion, which had a profound impact on the people of India and beyond, and Buddhism became one of the major religions of the world. Throughout his life, Buddha remained committed to his teachings and continued to spread his message of peace and compassion. Today, his teachings continue to inspire people around the world to seek inner peace and to cultivate qualities of compassion, kindness, and mindfulness in their lives.

After the Buddha became enlightened, Suddhodana experienced the struggle between tradition and change. He wanted his son to follow the customs of their kingdom. However, Siddhartha's path to enlightenment gave birth to a new religion that greatly influenced the course of history. Even though Suddhodana felt disappointed, he eventually understood and embraced his son's teachings. He even became a Buddhist himself and supported the spread of the religion throughout his kingdom. Although Siddhartha did not become a great king in the traditional sense, he became one of the most revered spiritual leaders in human history, whose teachings have impacted millions of lives around the world. Siddhartha Gautama, the Buddha, died at the age of eighty, having spent his life teaching and inspiring others. Today, his impact remains strong, with millions of people worldwide studying and practicing his teachings, ensuring his lasting legacy. The Buddha's philosophy has had a profound impact on the world, influencing not just religion but also philosophy, psychology, and science. His story is a testament to the power of human transformation and the potential for enlightenment and awakening within us all.

Buddha's Family

In his personal life, Siddhartha had an eventful marriage and formed a family of his own. When he was sixteen years old, their families arranged his marriage to Yasodhara, whom he had known since childhood. After their marriage, they lived a comfortable and privileged life in the palace. They had a son together named Rahula, a name that symbolized the concept of "fetter" or "hindrance." This name held significant meaning, reflecting Siddhartha's understanding that attachments and worldly desires can act as obstacles on the path to spiritual liberation. Despite the strong emotional bond between

Siddhartha and Yasodhara, his quest for enlightenment ultimately led him to leave behind his life as a prince, including his wife and child. Despite the eventual separation between Siddhartha and his family, the story of Rahula serves as a reminder of the challenges faced and the sacrifices made in pursuit of a higher spiritual calling. The story of Siddhartha's marriage to Yasodhara is often seen as a powerful example of the tension between traditional expectations and the desire for personal fulfillment. While Siddhartha was expected to follow in his father's footsteps and become a king, his spiritual journey took him in a completely different direction, causing him to break with tradition and pursue a new path. According to the legend, he left his home without saying goodbye to his family, keeping his departure a secret. In Buddhist tradition, it is believed that Rahula, his son, was born on the very day Siddhartha left the palace to embark on his spiritual journey in pursuit of enlightenment. Siddhartha's departure was a significant sacrifice for Yasodhara, as she had to continue her life without her husband by her side. Despite the difficult circumstances of their separation, she embraced the role of a devoted wife and single mother, waiting patiently for his return. Many years later, after Siddhartha attained enlightenment and became the Buddha, he reunited with Yasodhara and Rahula. Yasodhara, having witnessed her husband's transformation and understood the profundity of his teachings, became one of his most devoted followers. She became a nun and actively participated in the community of Buddhist monks and nuns. Although Siddhartha's journey towards enlightenment caused temporary separation from his family, his teachings and the example he set continue to inspire countless individuals around the world. The story of Siddhartha and Yasodhara's marriage serves as a reminder of the complexities of personal growth, sacrifice, and the pursuit of spiritual enlightenment.

Meanwhile, Rahula was raised in the palace with all the privileges and luxuries befitting a prince. However, when he was seven years old, his father returned to the palace as the Buddha and offered him the opportunity to become his disciple. He accepted and became the youngest monk in the Buddhist order. He was known for his intelligence and his devotion to his father's teachings. Rahula was said to have a particular talent for understanding complex philosophical concepts, and he was often called upon to explain the Buddha's teachings to others. Despite his young age, Rahula took his monastic vows seriously and practiced diligently. He is known to have asked his father for guidance on a number of occasions, and his father is said to have held him in high regard as a spiritual seeker. Rahula is also credited with several teachings of his own, including a discourse on the importance of mindfulness that is still studied and practiced by Buddhists today. In Buddhist tradition, Rahula is often held up as an exemplar of the monastic path and the importance of starting one's spiritual practice early in life. His life story also teaches us that one's spiritual journey can coexist harmoniously with family bonds. This is exemplified by his father's eventual reunion with his mother and him after attaining enlightenment.

In Buddhist tradition, the Buddha's relationship with his wife and child is often seen as an example of the impermanence and transience of all things. It is said that Siddhartha's decision to leave his family was motivated by his desire to end the cycle of suffering that he saw in the world. Nonetheless, the story also emphasizes the importance of love and compassion, and the Buddha's reunion with Yasodhara and Rahula after his enlightenment shows that spiritual pursuits need not preclude familial bonds. The Buddha is a profound example of enlightenment and spiritual awakening. His life and teachings serve as a source of inspiration and guidance for individuals seeking to cultivate inner peace, wisdom, and liberation. The Buddha's journey from a life of privilege and luxury to a renunciation seeking truth reflects the human capacity for transformation and the pursuit of ultimate truth. One key aspect that the Buddha exemplifies is the power of self-discovery and self-realization. Through his relentless quest for truth and his unwavering commitment to spiritual practice, the Buddha discovered the path to liberation and enlightenment. His example reminds us of the importance of self-exploration, introspection, and the willingness to question and challenge our assumptions and beliefs. Another valuable aspect of the Buddha's example is his emphasis on compassion and loving-kindness. The Buddha's teachings emphasize the cultivation of empathy, kindness, and compassion towards all beings. He showed that true happiness and fulfillment are found not only in our personal liberation but also in our ability to alleviate the suffering of others and contribute to the well-being of the world. Additionally, the Buddha's teachings highlight the significance of mindfulness and present-moment awareness. He emphasized the practice of mindfulness as a means to cultivate deep awareness and understanding of our thoughts, emotions, and experiences. The Buddha's example encourages us to live fully in the present moment, free from the burden of the past and the worries of the future.

In summary, the Buddha is a profound exemplar of enlightenment, self-discovery, compassion, and mindfulness. His life and teachings provide invaluable guidance and inspiration for those seeking personal growth, inner peace, and a deeper understanding of the nature of existence. By studying the Buddha's example, we can learn valuable lessons and incorporate these qualities into our own lives, fostering greater wisdom, compassion, and liberation. As we arrive at the last chapter, my deepest hope is that you all find meaningful and

THE BUDDHA SAID WHAT?!

transformative advice to carry with you. May these invaluable insights empower you to triumph over life's challenges while embarking on a heartfelt pursuit of a peaceful and harmonious existence.

155

GLOSSARY

Anatta	The doctrine of "non-self" or "no-self"
Asura	A type of supernatural being or deity that resides in one of the lower realms of existence within the cycle of rebirth
Atta	A concept of "self" or "soul", which is the counterpart of "anatta"
Cycle of Samsara	The cycle of birth, death, and rebirth, also known as the Wheel of Rebirth
Deva	A type of celestial being or deity that resides in higher realms of existence
Duggati	The realms of unfortunate or lower rebirth
Dukka	The inherent sense of dissatisfaction, impermanence, and unsatisfactoriness that characterizes life
Four Noble Truths	The fundamental truths about the nature of existence, the causes of suffering, and the path to liberation
Karma	The law of cause and effect states that our actions have consequences that shape our present and future experiences
Magga	A Pali word meaning "path" or "way," referring to the Noble Eightfold Path taught by the Buddha

Mahayana	A major branch of Buddhism, known as the "Great Vehicle"
Nirodna	A Pali word meaning "cessation" or "extinction", specifically referring to the end of suffering and the goal of liberation
Noble Eightfold Path	A central teaching in Buddhism, offering a path to end suffering and attain liberation
Preta	A type of supernatural being or realm known as "hungry ghosts"
Rebirth	The concept that after death, an individual's consciousness or soul is reborn into a new form of existence
Reincarnation	The concept that after death, an individual's consciousness or soul is reborn into a new body
Samatha	A Buddhist meditation practice that cultivates concentration, tranquility, and inner peace
Samudaya	The second noble truth, which explains the origin or cause of suffering
Suggati	The realm or state of fortunate rebirth
Theravada	One of the oldest surviving branches of Buddhism, primarily practiced in Sri Lanka, Myanmar, Thailand, Cambodia, and Laos
Vajrayana	A major branch of Buddhism practiced in Tibet, Bhutan, Nepal, and some parts of India, also called Tantric Buddhism or the Diamond Vehicle

Vipassana	A Buddhist meditation practice that cultivates mindfulness and deepens understanding of reality through clear insight

ACKNOWLEDGEMENTS

With heartfelt gratitude, I pen the closing words of this book, reflecting on the transformative journey it represents. The exploration of profound Buddhist teachings became a reality through the invaluable support, wisdom, and inspiration from countless individuals:

The Buddha, whose timeless wisdom guides seekers towards enlightenment, humbles me with its profound impact on countless lives.

My revered teachers and mentors, whose selfless guidance shaped this work and navigated the depths of Buddhist philosophy.

My beloved family, whose unwavering love and support provided the strength to complete this endeavor.

My friends and colleagues, whose encouragement sustained me through solitary writing sessions.

The insightful reviewers and diligent editors, whose contributions refined this book.

The dedicated publishing team, whose commitment to spreading Buddhist teachings is deeply appreciated.

The vibrant Buddhist communities worldwide, whose shared knowledge enriched my understanding.

The readers, both new and experienced practitioners, for whom I am honored to share these teachings.

As the journey continues beyond this book's pages, may its wisdom and compassion light the way toward understanding and peace for all beings.

With profound gratitude,
Anongpa Payanan

ABOUT THE AUTHOR

Anongpa is a native of Thailand, where Buddhism holds a dominant position. Her passion lies in writing books that explore Buddhist teachings and mindfulness to help readers find inner peace, navigate life's realities, and overcome obstacles. Through her insightful works, Anongpa guides readers on a transformative journey of self-discovery, offering practical wisdom to cultivate resilience and embrace the profound truths of existence. Her writings serve as a compassionate and relatable bridge between ancient teachings and the challenges of modern life, empowering readers to find solace and live harmoniously.

Made in the USA
Monee, IL
20 December 2023